PLAYING WITH A FULL DECK

52 Team Activities Using a Deck of Cards!

Michelle Cummings, M.S.

KENDALL/HUNT PUBLISHING COMPANY
4050 Westmark Drive   Dubuque, Iowa 52002

Dedicated to my King, Paul
and my two Jacks, Dawson and Dylan.

Cover image © Jupiter Images Corporation

Copyright © 2007 by Michelle Cummings

ISBN 13: 978-0-7575-4094-3
ISBN 10: 0-7575-4094-5

Kendall/Hunt Publishing Company has the exclusive rights to reproduce this work,
to prepare derivative works from this work, to publicly distribute this work.

Printed in the United States of America
10   9   8   7   6   5   4   3   2   1

Table of Contents

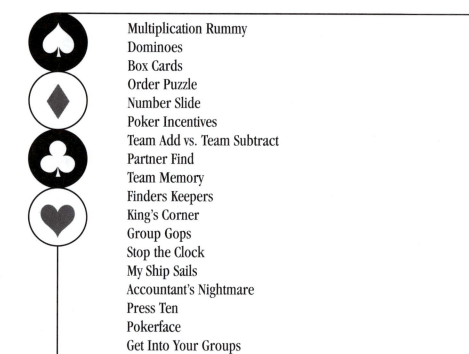

Welcome! A Note from Michelle

I've been hanging around Jokers most of my life, so it makes sense that I like playing cards! The first card games I remember playing as a kid were Nerts and Solitaire. Nerts was a competitive version of Solitaire that we played as a family all of the time. I had 5 siblings and a slew of cousins that lived nearby and during those long, cold winter days in Kansas we'd always play cards. Solitaires—There is something very satisfying in starting with disorder—a random arrangement of cards—and watching order restored, as the cards fall into a special pattern, change places according to a plan, or form an ordered sequence from Ace through King. There's a good metaphor there for life and anyone who works with groups.

A simple deck of cards can cover so much ground with any group that you work with. Everything from mixers and get to know you activities, problem solving initiatives, powerful diversity activities and great debriefing activities can all be done with a deck of cards. I like to use a 4" × 6" Jumbo deck of cards for any team activity as they are much easier to see in large groups. Most of the card activities in this book are geared towards groups of 10 or more, but there are some great ones you can do with small groups as well.

Throughout this book I used theories and work around multiple intelligences and the 7 Kinds of Smart work done by Thomas Armstrong and Howard Gardner. It is important that you examine the learning styles of your participants and choose activities that will match their strengths. If you select a wide variety of activities from multiple learning styles, each participant in your group will be engaged at different levels at different times. At the bottom of each activity it will note the learning style that is relevant for each activity.

In a traditional sit-around-a-table card game, your hands, eyes, and mind are all busy. Rules must be remembered and followed. All players are equal, whether adult or child, and there are winners and losers. In card games and solitaire, there is an element of suspense because the outcome is unpredictable. It's the result of skill, luck, or both.

A deck of cards is an amazing invention. Jut think about it . . . Cards from a standard deck can be divided in many ways—into red and black; suits (clubs, diamonds, hearts, and spades); and denominations (aces, twos, threes, etc.). The number cards (ace through ten) can be separated from the face cards, and the face cards, in turn, can be divided into men (jacks and kings) and women (queens).

Within the suits the numbers make it possible to order the cards from low to high or high to low.

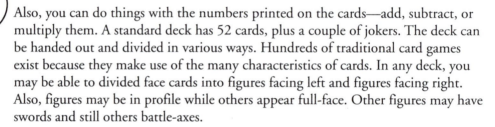

Also, you can do things with the numbers printed on the cards—add, subtract, or multiply them. A standard deck has 52 cards, plus a couple of jokers. The deck can be handed out and divided in various ways. Hundreds of traditional card games exist because they make use of the many characteristics of cards. In any deck, you may be able to divided face cards into figures facing left and figures facing right. Also, figures may be in profile while others appear full-face. Other figures may have swords and still others battle-axes.

Once you start using a deck of cards with groups you will wonder why you hadn't done it sooner! It is very important that you get all of your cards back at the end of each activity. As soon as you lose one card it can ruin several of the activities described. You also might ask your participants to handle them with care, i.e. no bending or folding the cards during play. If you need additional Jumbo card decks you can purchase them through the Training Wheels online store.

The Jokers in the deck can introduce some interesting dynamics in the group. Some are unsure of how to place a value on the Jokers so those cards sometimes get ignored or treated differently. All of these interactions are great to use in your debriefs after the activity.

When explaining the rules of the different card games in this book to your participants, you'll need to be clear and precise. The successful outcome of each activity is depending on it. You'll find yourself saying cue words like *first, then, before, after, under, over, behind, between, above.* Another key phrase I use often with groups while giving directions is, "In a minute but not yet. . . . .". This lets the group know they need to listen closely to the next set of directions, but not to move until they are told to do so. This phrase has helped me immensely with group control.

Card games engage players in classifying, ordering, reasoning, deducing, and devising strategies to solve a problem. These same skills help in science, math, and other studies. They help us concentrate, focus attention, hone motor skills, and become more sociable.

The first card activity I accidentally came up with was the Deck of Card Debrief, included here in this book.

I was working with at a wilderness camp for emotionally disturbed kids when one day a girl in my group decided to run away from camp. I was the staff member that followed her so she would not hurt herself or others. A good wilderness counselor always carries a first aid kit and a deck of cards with them. You just never know when you might need either one! When she finally got tired of walking we sat down in the woods. I told her I would wait until she was ready to talk about why she left the group. We waited, and waited, and waited. . . . . I got a little bored so I pulled out my deck of cards and started to play solitaire. She eventually started inching closer and closer to me so she could help me play. Then she asked if she could play a game. I made a deal with her that if she played a 'talking game' with me, then she could play one game of Solitaire before we returned to the group. I told her I would deal her 6 cards. We would each 'play' a card and have to share a story that coincided with the suit that was played. Each suit would have a different category. Diamonds represented positive attributes of herself. Clubs represented things going on at home she wanted to change, Spades were things that were preventing her from returning to the group, and Hearts represented any feelings she was having.

After hearing the categories she informed me (with the right amount of attitude) that she was not going to talk about her feelings if she was dealt any Hearts. I told her she didn't have to talk about her feelings if she was dealt any Diamonds, Clubs, or Spades. I shuffled the deck quite well, and I promise I did not stack the deck. She even cut the deck herself before I dealt out the hands. She was dealt 6 hearts. Now if we would have been playing poker she would have been quite excited, but needless to say, she was quite mad at her fate. She said many choice words and sat fuming for several minutes. Finally in a soft, small voice she said, "Maybe this is a sign that I need to talk about my feelings." Amazing! It was pretty awesome. We sat and talked for another hour before we returned to the group. I saw some pretty

significant changes in her over the next few weeks at camp. The right tool at the right time. . . . a deck of cards.

I hope you enjoy playing and facilitating the many games in this book. Also, try to expand your repertoire and knowledge of what cards offer. Ask other kids and adults from other regions or countries to teach you traditional card games. You'll find many similarities in games from around the world. Many of the activities in this book are twists on traditional playing card games.

Have fun out there,

Michelle

Michelle Cummings
Owner/Trainer/Big Wheel
Training Wheels

7 Kinds of Smart Information

Identifying and Developing Your Multiple Intelligences
By Thomas Armstrong, PH.D.

The activities in this e-book are written purposefully to include real life applications for the *7 Kinds of Smart*. Howard Gardner, originator of the theory of "multiple intelligences" suggests that thoughtful and intentional use of "The Seven Kinds of Smart" helps people to discover, unleash, honor and develop their intellectual strengths.

According to Dr. Armstrong these strengths are:

WORD SMART: Expressing your VERBAL intelligence

PICTURE SMART: Thinking with your mind's EYE

MUSIC SMART: Making the most of your MELODIC mind

BODY SMART: Using your KINESTHETIC intelligence

LOGIC SMART: Calculating your MATHEMATICAL and SCIENTIFIC abilities

PEOPLE SMART: Connecting with your SOCIAL SENSE

SELF SMART: Developing your INTRAPERSONAL intellect

As you read this e-book, the specific "kind of smart" being utilized will be noted near the bottom of each Activity page.

Primarily, this information is intended to feed the premise that we all have differing gifts (smarts) and if we can use them together "our whole will be greater than the sum of our parts." While participating in these activities, your participants may choose to "play to their strengths" or explore a secondary strength. Whatever they decide. . .

Celebrate your strengths!
Be optimistic about your weaknesses!

Adaptation used with permission from Faith Evans, PlayFully, Inc.
Original resource: Armstrong, Thomas. *The 7 Kinds of Smart*

Getting to Know a Deck of Cards

What's what and who's who in the deck?

There are fifty-two cards in the deck, plus two Jokers. The Jokers are not usually part of normal card playing games, but you will use them often in this book.

Sorting the Cards

You can sort the cards by Color: There are twenty-six red cards and twenty-six black cards in each deck. Hearts and Diamonds are always Red. Clubs and Spades are always black.

You can sort the cards by Suit: There are four suits: Hearts, Clubs, Diamonds, and Spades.

In each suit there are thirteen cards: Thirteen Hearts, Thirteen Diamonds, Thirteen Clubs, and Thirteen Spades.

You can sort the cards by Number or Letter: There are four of each number and letter—one card from each suit. There are four Aces, Four 2's, Four 3's and so on.

Each card has a number or a letter in the corner. The number cards have a number in the corner. Kings, Queens, and Jacks are called face cards. The Jack has a J. The Queen has a Q. The King has a K. The Ace has an A.

Each number card has the correct number of Hearts, Diamonds, Spades, or Clubs in the middle of the card.

A 2 of Hearts has two Hearts.
A 3 of Diamonds has three Diamonds.
A 5 of Clubs has five Clubs, and so on.

Poker Hands from Lowest to Highest

Although I'm not much of a gambler myself, there are a few activities in this book that will require the knowledge of the various hands in the game Poker. Here are some basic Poker hands and terminology.

In Poker, each player is dealt five cards. To win, you need certain combinations of cards in your hand. Here are the different Poker hands:

One Pair: Two matching cards. It doesn't matter what the other cards are. Example: K♣, 3♣, 5♣, 5♠, J♦

Two Pairs: Two sets of matching cards. Example: A♠, A♣, 3♣, 6♣, 6♦

Three of a Kind: Three matching cards. Example: Q♥, 8♥, 8♦, 8♠, A♣

Straight: Five Cards in order, but *not* all the same suit. Example: A♥, 2♣, 3♦, 4♣, 5♥. In a Straight, Aces may be high or low.

Flush: Five cards of the same suit, but not in any order. Example: K♥, J♥, 9♥, 5♥, 3♥

Full House: Three of a kind plus one pair—in any suits. Example: 3♠, 3♣, 7♦, 7♠, 7♣

Four of a Kind: Four matching cards. Example: Q♦, 8♠, 8♣, 8♦, 8♥

Straight Flush: Any five cards in the same suit *and* in order. Example: 2♦, 3♦, 4♦, 5♦, 6♦

Royal Flush: The 10, Jack, Queen, King, and Ace, all in the same suit. Example: 10♠, J♠, Q♠, K♠, A♠

Breaking a Tie in Poker
In traditional Poker, when players have the same kind of hand, whoever has the highest cards wins. Aces are high, except when they are used as 1's in a straight.

For example, if two players each have a hand that has two pairs. The first player has 4♣, 4♥, Q♠, 8♦, 8♣. The second player has 2♠, 2♣, 10♦, A♥, A♣. The second player wins because the pair of Aces is the highest pair between the two hands.

What if two hands are *exactly the same?* Then you must look at the suits. Hearts are highest, then Spades, then Diamonds, and Clubs are lowest.

If you have two hands that are straight flushes: 2♥, 3♥, 4♥, 5♥, 6♥ and 2♣, 3♣, 4♣, 5♣, 6♣. The hand with the hearts is the winner. Hearts are higher than spades.

Layout of This Book

The Activities in this book are coded by category so you can browse through and find the activity that will best suit your desired outcome. Below is the rationale behind each category and what type of activities you can find in each.

Get to Know You activities are great icebreakers and name games. They help ease the group into your program and get to know the people they are going to be doing activities with. They are usually lower risk activities that are more fun than anything else.

Energizer
The Energizer activities in the kit are designed to do just that. . . . Energize your groups! It is recommended to use Energizers at the beginning of your program to get the group in the right mindset of your program, but also as a 'pick me up' if you need to help change the energy within the group. Most of all, the Energizers are designed for you to have FUN!

Diversity
The collection of Diversity activities in this curriculum are powerful and considered higher risk activities compared to most of the other categories. These activities should be facilitated carefully and seriously. Children and adults need to learn about, appreciate, and experience their own culture and the cultures of others. An effective method of exploring other cultures is through structured activities.

Problem Solving
This section hosts a wide collection of problem solving initiatives. There is a nice selection of small group initiatives and large group problem solving activities.

Trust
Trust takes a long time to earn and only seconds to lose. This section focuses on trust within the group and how participants treat each other. These activities should be facilitated carefully and processed well.

Processing

This section will bring all of the other sections together for your participants. Processing helps make connections between educational experiences, real life and future learning. It helps participants apply the lessons they learn and skills they use in a "contrived environment" (i.e. your program), to real life issues such as resolving a conflict within a team or examining the communication styles of team members. Processing helps create purpose, meaning and focus of an activity. It helps participants take advantage of teachable moments.

Time Filler

This section is for those games that can fill some down time if you need to throw something in. There are some good lessons on playing fair, being safe, and following the rules. For the most part they're just plain fun!

ACTIVITIES

Card Mixers

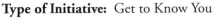

Type of Initiative: Get to Know You

Group Size: 2-104 participants

Playing the Game: The first 30 minutes of any program can really set the tone for your day. Getting your participants to connect with each other early on will alleviate any program jitters they might have coming into the day. As participants arrive to the program a good way for them to instantly connect with others in the group it to use a deck of cards. This activity can also serve as a way to debrief an activity.

Give each participant a card. Ask them to find a partner with a card that has something in common with their card. (this could be the suit, the number, or the color). You could have them discuss several things. Here are a few suggestions:

Get to Know You Topics:
• Find three things you have in common with your partner
• Share a goal you have for the day
• Share why you came to the program/workshop
• Discuss your favorite foods
• Describe the first car you ever owned

Debriefing Topics:
• Name 3 things you learned about one of your partners.
• How did you find your partner(s)? Did you rely on one method? (suit, color, or number?)
• Was it easy to share things about yourself?
• Discuss how you thought the group communicated during the day.
• Discuss who you thought the leader was in the last activity and why.

~self smart, people smart, word smart

Getting to Know You

Facilitator Notes:

Get It Back

Type of Initiative: Get to Know You

Group Size: 10–52 participants

Playing the Game: (idea from Diane Phillips)

Deal a Card to each player in the group—they can look at their card. Then ask them to simply mingle around meeting and greeting each other. You might tell players to share their name and their favorite food with each person they greet or any other appropriate information-seeking question. After each greet, players exchange Cards and then move along to find another person to meet and greet. After a minute or so you can call out, "Get It Back." Play continues in the same way as before except when a player receives their original Card, he can step out of the mingle and watch the rest of the players finish up the round. After all players have their original Card they should end up in a large circle. Then take a little time to find out how many names people remember.

Debriefing Topics:
• Name 3 things you learned about one of your partners.
• Did you come up with any strategies on how to get your own card back?
• Was it easy to share things about yourself?

-self-smart, people smart, word smart
Possiblesbag Teambuilding Kit Activity Manual, Chris Cavert.

Getting to Know You

Facilitator Notes:

Getting to Know You

Card Groupings

Type of Initiative: Get to Know You

Group Size: Best played with 16 or more players.

Setting Up the Cards: You'll want to arrange the Cards in order from Aces to Kings with each rank (number) in Hearts, Diamonds, Spades and Clubs, for example: the Aces are stacked Ace of Hearts, Ace of Diamonds, Ace of Spades, Ace of Clubs. Stack the twos the same way and the threes and so on through the deck.

Playing the Game: Deal out a Card, starting with the Aces, to each player in the group—ask them not to look at the face of the Card (if they accidentally do, have them exchange their Card with someone else in the group that already has a Card). When each player has a Card you will be asking the group to arrange themselves into smaller groups based on what you tell them. Players are not allowed to look at their Card and may not tell another player what his or her Card is in any way—players

may not "sign language" another players Card. Here is a suggested order:

1. Arrange yourselves into groups based on the color of your Card.
2. Arrange yourselves into 4 groups based on the suit of your Card.
3. Arrange yourselves into groups of like rank (number or face).
4. Arrange yourselves into pairs based on the like color and rank (use this one only if everyone will end up with a partner) or. . . . .
5. Arrange yourselves in order by suit and rank, Ace being the #1.

Getting to Know You

By ending with partners or small groups you can move into an activity that requires the resulting size. This is also a great way to break up any 'cliques' that may be in the group as the end result is very random. See the activity, **Cut the Deck,** on other ideas of how to split up a group.

Possibilities: You could ask the players to do a blind shuffle with 5 other players, meeting and greeting, before calling the next grouping—this throws off any hint of the Card they have. Also, since you were using the low numbers of the deck, moving into the activity, **What You Say,** works well.

Debriefing Topics:
• Was it hard not to look at your card? Why?
• How did the group help each other?
• What did it feel like once you were 'placed' into a group?

Facilitator Notes:

♣ A Little History

The earliest evidence of card playing has been found in China, with Central Asia soon following suit (if you'll pardon the pun). The first cards were simple paper dominoes found in China. Europe got its first taste of the new craze in the 14th century when Islamic-influenced packs, complete with court cards, appeared in Italy and Spain. We know that card games arrived in Europe at around this time because soon afterwards several courts in Italy and Switzerland outlawed the playing of such heretical games.

~self smart, people smart, picture smart
Possiblesbag Teambuilding Kit Activity
Manual, Chris Cavert

Getting to Know You

What You Say

Type of Initiative: Get to Know You

Group Size: Plays well with 6-8 players in a group—multiple groups can play.

Setting Up the Cards: You'll need the low Cards of the Deck, 6 and below.

Playing the Game: (shared at the TERA conference, **T**exas **E**xperiential **R**opes **A**ssociation). Deal one card to every player. You will ask the members of the group to share one thing about themselves for every number on their Card—4 of Hearts, four things about themselves. You could get more specific by asking a question like, "Tell us things you like to do" or "Places you have been outside the state." In between

questions have your participants trade cards with 3 people in their small group so they have a different number of items to share each time.

Possibilities: Each player could choose another player in the group to answer a question. For example, if I am holding the 3 of Clubs, I will ask Steve, "Tell us 3 things about yourself we cannot tell by looking at you." After Steven has answered he will get to ask the next question. Each player will ask and answer one question. If I have the 4 of Hearts, I ask you, "Tell me four things you like to do on vacation," (Mine: Spend time with family, try new foods, swim in the ocean, or hike in the woods).

Variations: Leave the high cards in the deck! The face cards will have a value of 10 and the Ace can be a 1 or an 11. It's interesting in the real world today how very little we share about ourselves with others. Leaving the high cards in the deck will 'force' someone into sharing more things about themselves.

Debriefing Topics:
• Tell the group something new you learned about your partner.
• Was it difficult to share so many things about yourself?

Facilitator Notes:

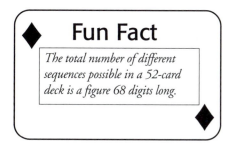

Fun Fact

The total number of different sequences possible in a 52-card deck is a figure 68 digits long.

-self smart, people smart, picture smart, word smart
Possiblesbag Teambuilding Kit Activity Manual, Chris Cavert

Cut the Deck

Type of Initiative: Splitting the Group Up/Group Management

Group Size: 10-52 participants

Playing the Game: There are several ways to divide your groups with a deck of cards. This could be introduced at any time during your program. Many times when you work with a larger group of people, there are mini-cliques already formed. Here are some creative ways to encourage your participants to meet others and get to know more about those they are not as close with.

And let's face it, there are some people you just don't want to have in the same group! Here are some creative ways to split up the group using a deck of cards.

1. Odds and Evens
   - Using the entire deck: 52 cards, 28 odds, 24 evens (Aces = 1, Jacks = 11, Queens = 12, Kings = 13)
   - Take out the Royalty cards: 40 cards, 20 odds, 20 evens (Aces = 1)
   - Each suit: 13 cards, 7 odds, 6 evens
   - Two suits: 26 cards, 14 odds, 12 evens
   - Three suits: 39 cards, 21 odds, 18 evens
   - Each suit without royalty cards: 10 cards, 5 odds, 5 evens

2. Color of the Cards
   - Full deck: 52 cards, 26 black cards, 26 red cards
   - Hearts: 13 red cards
   - Spades: 13 black cards
   - Diamonds: 13 red cards
   - Clubs: 13 black cards

3. Suit of the Cards
   - Full deck: 52 cards, 4 suits (hearts, spades, diamonds, and clubs) 13 per group
   - Two suits: 26 cards, 13 per group

Getting to Know You

4. Number or face value of the Cards
   - Full deck: 52 cards, groups of 4 (four 9's, four Jacks)
   - Three suits: 39 cards, groups of 3 (three 7's, three Aces)
   - Two suits: 26 cards, pairs (two 3's, two Queens)

5. Pairs based on the like color and rank (use this one only if everyone will end up with a partner)
   - Full deck: 52 cards, 26 pairs of people (2 of diamonds and 2 of hearts)

Facilitator Notes:

♣ A Little History

The deck of cards is sometimes likened to an almanac. The 52 cards remind us that there are 52 weeks in a year; 12 face cards suggest the 12 months of the year. Four suits suggest the four seasons of the year. And if we add up all the spots in a deck of cards—one for Ace, two for a two, three for a three, and so on up to 11 for a Jack, 12 for a Queen, and 13 for a King, and one more for a Joker—then we get the total of 365, the number of days in a year.

Getting to Know You

-people smart, body smart

4 of a Kind

Type of Initiative: Get to Know You, Energizer

Group Size: Best played with 16 or more players.

Setting Up the Cards: You will need one card for each participant with 3-4 cards from each suit. For example, if you have 13 people in your group you would need four Diamonds, four Hearts, three Clubs, and three Spades.

Playing the Game: Invite your group to stand in a circle. Shuffle the cards and deal each participant one card. Ask them to hold it face down and not look at their card. The goal of the activity is for participants get into groups of 4 according to suits as quickly as possible. When the facilitator calls out, "Go!" participants quickly look at their card and scramble to get into 4 of a kind. When a group believes they are in the right place they put their finger next to their nose. After groups have formed, they must come up with 4 things they all have in common with each other. After a few minutes of sharing, all groups exchange cards with three people from other groups so they do not know what card they have. When the facilitator calls out "Go!" participants quickly look at their card and scramble to get into 4 of a kind.

Variation: When the facilitator calls out "Go!" participants place their card to their forehead without looking at it. Group members must help each other get into 4 of a kind.

Debriefing Topics:
• What were some of the things you found you had in common with others in the group?
• Was is difficult to find four things you have in common?

**♣ A Little History**

When American astronauts orbited Earth, they took special fireproof playing cards with them.

♣

-self smart, people smart, picture smart

Getting to Know You

Facilitator Notes:

Getting to Know You

Alliteration Anticipation

Type of Initiative: Time Filler

Group Size: Best played with 6-12 players.

Playing the Game: Invite your group to stand or sit in a circle. Deal each participant one card and ask them to hold it face down. The participant to the facilitator's left begins by saying, "I went to the department store and I bought. . . . ." As soon as he has said "bought", the participant to the facilitator's right shows their card. The participant who is speaking must immediately say the number of the turned-up card and a noun that begins with the same letter as the number of the card.

For example, for a two he might say, "two tangerines"; for a four, "four firecrackers." For an ace, instead of "one," the player uses "an" and so might say, "an avocado." For face cards, no number is used, simply the first letter of the card. So, for a jack, the player might say, "a jellybean"; for a queen, "a quince"; and for a king, "a kite."

Play continues all the way around the circle. The second time around the circle the participants must precede the noun with an adjective. For example: "five fine forks," "ten tiny turnips," "a quaint quilt, " etc.

Variations: To encourage further vocabulary building, vary the carrier sentence: "I went to the zoo and saw. . . . ." or "I went to the toy store and bought. . ."

Please feel free to specify the phrase to fit your group. For example:

I went to camp and I took. . . . . . Two tarps, three thermometers, four frogs, an air mattress. . . .

I went to school and I took. . . . Two tablets, three thumbtacks, four fractions, an apple . . .

I went on a backpack trip and I took. . . . . Two tents, three thermoses, four forks, an ant trap

I went on a corporate retreat and I took. . . . Two tables, three theories on management, four fur coats, an apprentice . . .

I went into rehab and I took. . . . . Two tube socks, three therapists, four family photos, an angry attitude. . . .

Time Filler

To elicit verbs instead of nouns, use this sentence: "My grandmother told me never to. . . ." This can be made more difficult by requiring players to add two alliterative words—here, a verb and an adverb, or a verb and a noun. Participants will begin to see the differences between verbs that are transitive (requiring an object) and those that are intransitive.

Some examples of sentences produced in this variation of the game follow. Two words finish the sentence. "My grandmother told me never to. . . ."

Ace	act angry
Two	tease turtles
Three	throw tantrums
Four	faint foolishly
Five	fall fast
Six	swallow sardines
Seven	speak sarcastically
Eight	eat eels
Nine	nibble nuts
Ten	terrify tarantulas
Jack	joke jovially
Queen	quit quoting
King	kick kittens

Learning Skills: practice in phonics (initial sounds of words), verbal fluency, understanding of sentence structure and parts of speech, sensitivity to alliteration.

Debriefing Topics:
• What was difficult about this activity for you?
• Was this harder than you thought it would be? Why or why not?

Facilitator Notes:

~self smart, people smart, picture smart, word smart, logic smart
Reference: Idea from Margie Golick, Card Games for Smart Kids.

Time Filler

Killer Wink

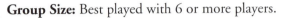

Type of Initiative: Time Filler

Group Size: Best played with 6 or more players.

Setting Up the Cards: This is an age old party game. You will use playing cards to determine who is the 'killer.' You will need one card per person, with one Ace card as one of the cards.

Playing the Game: Invite your participants to sit or stand in a circle. Hand each participant a card and ask them to look at it but not show it to anyone. If someone receives the Ace, he/she is the killer for that round. The object is for the killer to catch someone's eye and wink at them. The leader starts the game by saying, "Go!". Participants mingle around the play area trying to find the killer. The killer tries to kill everyone by carefully winking at a person when he has their eye contact. He does not want anyone else to see him wink. If a player is winked at, he does a great theatrical death scene within 5 seconds of being winked at. If someone thinks he knows who the killer is, he points at him/her and says, "I accuse __Ashley__ !" If he is correct, he wins and the game is over. Otherwise, both he and Ashley are out of the game.

Debriefing Topics:
• What made this activity fun?
• Did everyone play fair? How does playing fair make activities more enjoyable?

-people smart, body smart

Time Filler

Facilitator Notes:

Chase the Ace

Type of Initiative: Time Filler

Group Size: Best played with 6 or more players.

Playing the Game: Invite your participants to stand in a circle. Deal out a single card to each player, face down. Randomly choose one person to start the activity and call them the dealer.

The player with the lowest card (aces are low) will receive a letter 'A'. The activity is over when the first person spells out the word "ACE."

Now each player looks at his card. Each player has to decide whether his card is high enough to keep him in the game. If the player thinks it is, he will say "stand" (stick with his card). If a player thinks his card is too low, he will say "Exchange," and pass the card, face down, to the player on his left, who must accept it and give him his card in return. This process continues around the circle until play comes back to the dealer.

If the dealer is not happy with his card, he gives it back to the facilitator who replaces it at the bottom of the pack and gives him another card. Next, all players show their cards. The player with the lowest card receives the letter 'A'. The activity is over when the first person spells out the word "ACE."

Cards are then reshuffled and re-dealt, and the same process is repeated. If two or more players tie for lowest card, each receives a letter.

Special rule: if you are dealt a king, you neither stand nor exchange. Place your Card Face up in front of you, and relax for the rest of the round.

Debriefing Topics:
• What did you like about this activity?
• How did you attempt to mask what card you had?
• Was it difficult to decide whether to 'stand' or 'exchange'?

~logic smart, people smart

Time Filler

Facilitator Notes:

♣ A Little History

There are playing cards useful for travelers. Each card in the pack teaches a phrase in several foreign languages. In one deck, the Six of Diamonds gives the translation of "Where can I get a taxi?" in Spanish, French, and German: "¿Donde puedo encontrar un taxi?" "Où est-ce que je peux trouver un taxi?" "Wo kann ich hier ein Taxi bekommen bitte?"

♣

Time Filler

Prediction

Type of Initiative: Time Filler, Consensus Building

Group Size: Best played with 2 or more players.

Aim of the Game: To turn over all 52 cards in a deck without predicting one correctly.

Playing the Game: Invite your group to sit or stand in a circle. This can be a lengthy game so make sure they are comfortable. Small groups of 5-6 is recommended.

Shuffle the deck and hand it to one person in the group. Explain that before turning over the first card, the person holding the cards must announce a rank of card. For example, 'Five.' They must say the word out loud and be clear. The goal is to try to avoid predicting the card they are about to turn over. If the announcement coincides with the rank of card revealed, the game is immediately over. So if they announced, 'Six' and then turned over the six of diamonds, the game is over. Then the cards can be shuffled and the game recommences with the next participant.

The game continues in this way until they either predict a card or you get through the entire deck. This latter situation is extremely rare. This game is also made harder by the rule that you cannot make the same prediction in consecutive turns.

Variation: To use as a consensus building game, ask the group to come to consensus on the number they are predicting before turning the card over. This takes a lot longer to play, but can help build the suspense of what card is being turned over if the entire group is responsible for the number. It's quite fun to hear the whole group squeal with "Ooohhh's" and "Aaaaah's" if they predict a ten card and a nine card is revealed, or with other cards that are close to the predicted number.

-logic smart, picture smart, people smart

Time Filler

Facilitator Notes:

In Devonshire, England, you'll find an inn called the Pack O' Cards Inn. It was built in the 17th century to celebrate the owner's luck at gambling. The inn has four floors, 52 windows, and 13 doors.

Time Filler

The Conductor

Type of Initiative: Time Filler, Consensus Building

Group Size: Best played with 12 or more players.

Aim of the Game: To conduct a song using the sounds of the cards.

Playing the Game: (Learned at an AEE conference using clapping instead of cards, conducted by Craig Dobkin)

Divide your group into 4-5 smaller groups. Deal one card to each participant. Instruct them that whenever you point at their group, they need to slap their card on their hand in unison. Only the group you point at should make the noise, the other groups wait until you point to them. They should slap their card to their hand one time for each time you point to their group. So if you point to a group three times in a row, they should slap their card to their hand three times in a row.

As the facilitator, get creative and animated when pointing to different groups. Come up with a familiar song that they might recognize as they are slapping their cards to your directions. Children's Songs such as Row, Row, Row Your Boat or Mary Had a Little Lamb are easy songs to conduct.

Facilitator Notes:

-music smart, body smart, people smart

Time Filler

War

Type of Initiative: Energizer

Group Size: Best played with 10 or more players.

Setting Up the Game: Divide the group into even teams. Lay a piece of rope or webbing on the ground. Have one group stand on one side of the line, the other group on the other side of the line.

Playing the Game: This game is a variation from the common game Giants, Wizards, and Elves and a twist on the traditional card game War. In the traditional game of War, players sit around a table and the entire deck of cards is dealt out to two people. Players do not look at their cards, which are placed face down in a pack in front of them. Both players simultaneously turn over the top card in their respective piles and place it face up in the middle of the table. The highest-rank card wins the hand and collects the cards, placing them face down at the bottom of his or her pack. Aces are high and suits are ignored. If the two cards played are of equal value, the two players must now go to War. They both now place the top cards of their packs face down in the middle of the table. These cards are not revealed; instead, the players return to their packs and take the new top card, turning it over and placing it face up on the table. Whoever plays the highest card wins the hand and collects all six cards from the middle of the table, which are placed face down at the bottom of his or her pack. The winner of this game is the person who collects all 52 cards, leaving their opponent with nothing.

So for the group version of War, divide the group into even teams. Lay a piece of rope or webbing on the ground. Have one group stand on one side of the line, the other group on the other side of the line. Give each participant a card and ask them not to look at it. Players from each team approach the line and face off against one player from the other team. If there are uneven teams, those without a person to face off against must wait until the next round to play. Inform the group whether Aces will be high or low. On the count of three each pair will reveal their card simultaneously to their partner. Whoever has the higher card wins their opponent to their side. If players reveal the same card they

declare a tie and both members remain on their own side. Then players exchange cards with at least three people on their side so they do not know what card they have. Then play resumes as stated above. Players from each team approach the line and face off against one player from the other team. Play continues as long as participants are still having fun!

War (*Continued*)

Learning Skills: Understanding concepts of higher and lower

Facilitator Notes:

-people smart, logic smart, body smart

Zero War

Type of Initiative: Energizer

Group Size: Best played with 10 or more players.

Setting Up the Game: Divide the group into even teams. Lay a piece of rope or webbing on the ground. Have one group stand on one side of the line, the other group on the other side of the line.

Object of the Game: The object of Zero War is to be on the team with the most players at the end of the game.

Point Value of Cards:
Cards are equal to their face value.

- Jack = 11 points
- Queen = 12 points
- Kings = 13 points
- Ace = 1 point

Black cards have a positive value (+).

Red cards have a negative value (−).

Playing the Game: Give each participant a card and ask them not to look at it. Two players from each team approach the line and show their cards simultaneously, as in the game War. The pair whose total value is closest to zero (0) wins their opponents to their side.

For example, if Team A has the Four of Spades and the Queen of Diamonds (+4 and −12 = −8) and Team B has the Four of Diamonds and King of Clubs (−4 and +13 = +9), then Team A is the winner and the pair from Team B changes sides. In the case of a tie (say, Team A has +2 and Team B has −2), then each pair remains on their team and two new players approach the line.

Learning Skills: Adding and subtracting negative numbers.

Facilitator Notes:

-people smart, logic smart, body smart

Problem Solving

Energizer

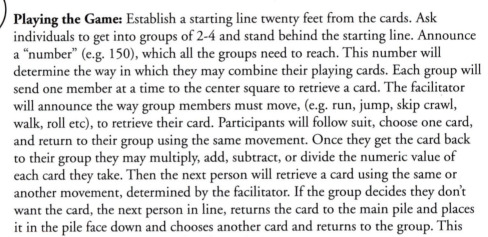

Take One

Type of Initiative: Energizer, Problem Solving

Group Size: Best played with 10 or more players.

Props Needed: Rope barrier for Cards, Deck of Playing Cards

Setting Up the Cards: Place a rope on the ground in a square. Place the entire deck of cards face down in the square. For large groups use multiple decks of cards. The 2-10 cards will equal their face value. Aces equal 1 or 11. Kings, Queens and Jacks have a value of 10.

Playing the Game: Establish a starting line twenty feet from the cards. Ask individuals to get into groups of 2-4 and stand behind the starting line. Announce a "number" (e.g. 150), which all the groups need to reach. This number will determine the way in which they may combine their playing cards. Each group will send one member at a time to the center square to retrieve a card. The facilitator will announce the way group members must move, (e.g. run, jump, skip crawl, walk, roll etc), to retrieve their card. Participants will follow suit, choose one card, and return to their group using the same movement. Once they get the card back to their group they may multiply, add, subtract, or divide the numeric value of each card they take. Then the next person will retrieve a card using the same or another movement, determined by the facilitator. If the group decides they don't want the card, the next person in line, returns the card to the main pile and places it in the pile face down and chooses another card and returns to the group. This continues until the group reaches the goal.

Variations:
- Instead of the facilitator calling out the movements, allow the individual to decide what movements they will make each time to the center square. Every time an individual goes out to get a card they have to move in a different way going and returning to their group.
- Only allow a limited number of mathematical functions (e.g. Use addition only, use addition and subtraction only, etc.)
- Have each group come up with a "cheer" using a word, sound, and movement when they reach the goal.

Debriefing Topics:
• How did you strategize during this game?
• Were all of the suggestions heard?
• Did anyone feel left out?
• Did you discover something about another individual in your group?
• How did you all work together?

Facilitator Notes:

♣ A Little History

Card decks that can be used by people with up to 95 percent visual impairment are available. The numbers on them are twice the size of the numbers on conventional playing cards, and two additional colors—blue and green—are used to help players who are unable to distinguish the suit markings.

-logic smart, body smart, music smart, self smart
Created by Mary Ann Loeffler

Problem Solving

Energizer

In-Between

Type of Initiative: Energizer

Group Size: Best played with 9 or more players.

Setting Up the Cards: You will need one card for each participant. A random selection of cards is best.

Playing the Game: Invite your group to stand in a circle. Shuffle the cards and deal each participant one card. Ask them to hold it face down and not look at their card. The goal of the activity is for participants get into groups of 3 with the number card in the middle being in-between the two outer numbers as quickly as possible. When the facilitator calls out, "Go!" participants quickly look at their card and scramble to get into the correct group. When a group believes they are in the right place they put their finger next to their nose. After the first round, participants exchange cards with three people from other groups so they do not know what card they have. When the facilitator calls out "Go!" participants quickly look at their card and scramble to get into the correct group.

This activity plays well with 4 of a Kind.

Learning Skills:
• Understanding concepts of "in between," "higher," and "lower"
• Calculating probabilities

Facilitator Notes:

-people smart, logic smart, body smart

Energizer

Medieval Evolution

Type of Initiative: Energizer

Group Size: Best played with 12 or more players.

Playing the Game: It has been said that the four suit symbols originally represented the four classes of society in Medieval Europe. Spades represented the Nobles, Hearts the Clergy, Diamonds the Merchants, and Clubs the Peasants and Serfs. This ranking (spades, hearts, diamonds, and clubs), from the highest to the lowest, still holds in the popular card game Bridge. For the purpose of this game each class of society will have a different action.

♣ Peasants: Since peasants were often seen cleaning out the pig pen, the action to represent a Peasant will be shoveling of pig manure and tossing over one's shoulder.

♦ Merchants: Since merchants were often handling money and self employment is definitely a gamble, the action to represent a Merchant will be to pull down on slot machine handle and say, "Cha-Ching!"

♥ Clergy: Clergy were always praying, so the action to represent a Clergy will be to walk with hands in a prayer position and bow to one another.

♠ Nobles: Nobles were the royals. So for a royal to find another royal, they must hold one hand up in the air, sachet around the group and say, "You're not worthy! You're not worthy!"

Process: Each person in the group is dealt a small stack of 5 cards. Ask them not to look at the card. Everyone in the group will start out as a Peasant. A Peasant will do the Peasant action to find another Peasant. Once they have found one another, they will count to three and reveal their top card to their opponent. The first Peasant to add up the two cards and shout out the correct answer advances to a Merchant. The Peasant who lost that round, remains a Peasant and must find another Peasant to

continue play. Players move the card used in play to the bottom of their small deck. Then the Merchant will do the Merchant action to find another Merchant. On the count of three they will show their card to their opponent. The first Merchant to add up the two cards and shout out the correct answer advances to a Clergy, The Merchant who lost that round, remains a Merchant, and so on.

When a Noble challenges another Noble, whoever wins becomes a Joker, after all, this is a silly game! Whoever loses remains a Noble. All of the Jokers will congregate together and tell each other bad "Knock Knock" jokes. This continues until you have many Jokers and you decide to end the game.

Sample Knock Knock Jokes:

• "Knock Knock", "Who's there?" "Dwyane" "Dwyane who?" "Dwayne the bathtub I'm dwowning!"
• "Knock Knock", "Who's there?" "Boo." "Boo who?" "Don't cry, it's only a joke!"

Facilitator Notes:

~body smart, word smart, logic smart, picture smart, people smart

Pair Tag-Quad Tag

Type of Initiative: Energizer

Group Size: Best played with 12 or more players.

Setting Up the Cards: You will need two cards of like value (i.e. two 5 cards, two Kings, two 9 cards). Each participant will receive one card. This game is best played with an even number of participants.

Playing the Game: Invite your group to stand in a circle. Hand everyone a card. Each person may look at their card and then hold it facing out so everyone else in the circle can see their card, too. Without changing places, have participants scan the circle to find the participant with the same number card that they have. This will be their partner.

Have one participant decide who will be 'it' first and who will be 'chased' first. Remind your participants that this is a fast walking game. When the facilitator says "Go!" the person who is 'it' walks fast towards the person being 'chased'. As in a normal tag game the person being 'chased' tries to avoid getting tagged by the person who is 'it'.

If the person being chased is tagged by the 'it' then they reverse roles. The person who WAS being chased is now IT and must turn around in a circle before fast walking after their partner.

Can be used in small groups or groups as large as 1,000!

Variation: Quad Tag
After you have played Pair Tag, you can easily move into Quad Tag. Have your Pairs stand together with their cards and link elbows. You will have to exchange half of the group's cards with new cards that match the other half of the group's cards. Example: If you have 16 participants you will have 8 pairs of people linked at the elbow. Four groups will keep their cards. You will exchange the other four groups with cards that match the first four groups. To begin play, the pairs will find the other pair in the circle that have the same cards as they do. One group will start as 'it' and the other pair will be 'chased' first. Same rules apply as above.

Debriefing Topics:
• Was it difficult to find your partner amongst all of the other people?
• What strategies did you come up with to avoid getting tagged? to tag your partner?

~people smart, body smart

Energizer

Facilitator Notes:

Energizer

♣ A Little History

Some card decks feature useful tips, like cards with first-aid instruction or outdoor survival hints for campers in the wild.

The King Is Coming!

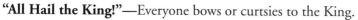

Type of Initiative: Energizer

Group Size: Best played with 12 or more players.

Setting up the Cards: You will need at least three cards of each numeric value, (e.g. 3 ten cards, 3 nine cards, 3 four cards, etc). Each participant will receive one card.

Playing the Game: This is a variation from Sam Sikes' game, The Captain is Coming. It is a great ice breaker and energizer for any group larger than 10 . . . preferably larger than 20. The facilitator plays the role of the King/Queen and is the person who calls out the orders. The following orders are several actions that the group does during the game depending on what the King/Queen calls out:

"All Hail the King!"—Everyone bows or curtsies to the King.

"Pair"—Everyone finds one person who has the same number of card that they do. Example: 4 of spades and 4 of diamonds. Option #1: they conduct a sword fight with one another. Option #2: They dance together at the King's ball. Use whichever one fits your group better.

"3 of a Kind"—Everyone gets into a group of three cards with the same numeric value. Example: 3 of hearts, 3 of diamonds, 3 of spades. This group must raise the drawbridge! One person stands in the middle and uses their arms as the planks of the drawbridge. The other two stand on each side of the drawbridge planks and crank them up.

"Two Pair"—Everyone gets into a group of four cards that makes up two pairs of cards. Example: two 5 cards and two Jacks. This group must stand in a line and do the Riverdance!

"Flush"—Everyone gets into a group of five cards of the same suit. Example: 3,6,7,9,Jack of Spades. This group stands in a tight huddle with their backs to one another, pretends to flush a toilet, and makes a "Whoosh" sound.

Energizer

"Straight"—Everyone gets into a group of five cards with a numeric run. Example: 7,8,9,10,Jack. This group of five quickly stands in a straight line in the correct numeric order with arms folded as if they were in straight jackets.

For people who cannot get into a group before the facilitator blows his/her whistle, they must "Leave the Kingdom!" These people walk over to a designated area and sing and dance to a Jester's song. "I've got a lovely bunch of coconuts. . . . ." (repeat over and over and over and over. . . . . . .)

Joker's Wild!—This command allows all participants who have had to "Leave the Kingdom!" to re-enter the game.

Variation: After each command is called out, have each participant trade cards with three people. Ask them not to look at their card. When the command is called out they can quickly look at their new card and get into the correct group.

Facilitator's Notes:

~people smart, body smart, logic smart

Energizer

Sentence Shuffle

Type of Initiative: Problem Solving

Group Size: Best played with 5 or more players. Small groups of 5-6 is recommended.

Aim of the Game: The object of Sentence Shuffle is to line up the cards in "sentences." In this game, cards have an alphabetical value, rather than a numerical one. Each card stands for the first letter of its name.

That means, Ace = A, King = K, Queen = Q, Jack = J, Two = T, Three = T, Four = F, etc.

Playing the Game: Divide the team into smaller groups of 5-6. Deal each participant a card. Ask them to keep their card and not trade it with anyone. Each group must compose a sentence using their cards using alphabetical values. Participants must stand in the correct order and present their sentence to the larger group.

For example, one group of 6 participants is dealt an ace, three, two, king, four, and a seven. Their sentence might be, "A tiny taupe kangaroo falls softly."

Encourage each group to come up with 3 or 4 sentences. Have them pick their favorite sentence to present to the large group.

Sample Sentences:
Four—Queen—Two—Six—Seven:
  "Father quit the Secret Service."

Eight—Three—Seven—Five—Six:
  "Eat the soup for supper."

Debriefing Topics:
• What made this activity unique?
• How did your group work together to come up with your sentences?
• Who was the leader in your group?

-word smart, people smart, logic smart

Problem Solving

Facilitator Notes:

♠U.S. Influences

According to many experts, card players have the United States to thank for refining playing cards. Americans are apparently responsible for rounding the corners of our cards and adding varnish to make them more durable. The US influence is also reputed to be responsible for making the court cards double-headed and inventing jokers (though this is not without some dissent).

Get 20

Type of Initiative: Problem Solving

Group Size: Best played with 5 or more players.

Playing the Game: Invite your participants to get into groups of 4 or 5. Give each participant one card. Ask them to use any math function (addition, subtraction, multiplication and division) to get their cards into a sequence that would equal the number 20. For example, if one group had a cluster of cards that are these values: a King(10), Ace (1 or 11), 5, 6 and 8, the group would get into a line and explain to the group how they equal 20: a King plus an Ace would be 11, 11 plus 8 equals 19, 19 plus 6 equals 25. 25 minus 5 equals 20. Occasionally you will have groups that will not be able to make their cards work for a value of 20. In this case you can invite other groups to invite a 'card' to their group and make a new sequence. You can also exchange cards with the group so they have new numbers to work with. If a group is able to 'Get 20' quickly, challenge them to see how many different equations they can come up with using the same cards. Some groups have been able to come up with 6 or more equations! This allows groups to continue working even if they are 'done.' This will also allow those groups that are not as quick to have the time they need to be successful at finding their equation. After each group has at least one equation that will equal 20, ask them to choose their favorite equation. Each group can then present their equation to the large group.

Debriefing Topics:
• How did your group work together to come up with 20?
• Were you able to come up with more than one solution?
• How did you involve everyone in your group?
• Who was the leader in your group? What leadership qualities did they immolate?

~logic smart, body smart, people smart

Problem Solving

Facilitator Notes:

Group Blackjack
Group Jackblack

Type of Initiative: Problem Solving

Group Size: Best played with 12 or more players.

Playing the Game: Invite your participants to get into a large circle. Give each participant a card and ask them not to look at it. (In case someone peeks at their card, have them trade cards with their neighbor.) Inform the group that this is a silent activity and they may not use their voices for the duration of the activity. Ask them to place their card to their forehead so it is visible to the rest of their team. Instruct them to play 'Blackjack' as a large group. Using addition only, each participant must be included in a 'hand' that equals a combined value of 19, 20, or 21.

Here are some simple blackjack rules in case you are unfamiliar with them: Aces equal a value of 1 or 11. Royalty cards equal a value of 10. All other number cards are face value. When given a range of 19, 20, and 21 group members should be able to include EVERYONE in the group no matter how many participants you have. Even groups of 15 should be able to complete the task as long as you deal a few aces.

Suggestion: Throw a Joker card in and make it a 'wild' card, so it can be whatever value they want it to be.

Variation: Group Jackblack! (No, not the actor) The object of Jackblack is to subtract points, rather than adding them. Instead of trying to get into groups totaling 19, 20, or 21 as in Group Blackjack, participants start with 21 and subtract card totals to get into groups that total 0, 1, or 2.

Problem Solving

Debriefing Topics:
• How did you get into your groups?
• Did anyone feel left out?
• How did it feel when someone helped you find a partner?

Facilitator Notes:

~logic smart, body smart, picture smart, people smart

52 Card Pickup

Type of Initiative: Problem-Solving

Group Size: Best played with 12 or more players.

Playing the Game: This is a great large group activity. Set 4 chairs back to back in a square fashion so that each line protrudes out from the center like the spokes of a wheel. Designating which chair is for which suit is optional. One way to start it is to give each participant a card and tell them not to look at it. Tell them that whoever has the king in each suit is to sit in the chair. Then the queen on his/her lap, then the jack on the queen's lap, etc. You will eventually have one big lap sit! Once everyone has been given a card tell them to look at it and then line up in order by suit as quickly as possible. Be ready for loud and fast! Another way to start the activity is to give the instructions first and then fling the cards up in the air and let them scramble for a card and then line up.

Variation: Timing this activity is a good way to let groups see improvement. Establish a baseline time and challenge the group to get their "best" time by improving the process.

Variation: Another variation is to do this activity silently and without looking at their cards. After you deal a card to each individual, ask them to place it to their forehead without looking at the card. Then without talking have them figure out which king sits in which chair and the chaos begins!

If the chairs described above are an issue, ask the group to create a square shape with each suit at one side.

Variation: In the middle of a circled group of players, spread the Cards out face down. The challenge is to see how fast the group can line up all the suits in order—Ace to King—ending up with a square of players. Ask the group to create a square shape with each suit at one side, each player holding up at least 2 cards. (If there are not enough hands you can let the players line the Cards up in a square on the floor.) Establish a baseline time and challenge the group to get their "best" time by improving the process.

Variation: Once the Cards are nice and broken in, you could provide a dramatic start to either variation described above by tossing the Cards into the air, letting them hit the ground before you say, "GO!"

52 Card Pickup (*Continued*)

Debriefing Topics:
- How successful do you think you were at this activity?
- Was there any confusion on where you were supposed to go?
- How did timing the activity make a difference in your performance?

Facilitator Notes:

~picture smart, logic smart, body smart
Possiblesbag Teambuilding Kit Activity Manual, Chris Cavert pg. 36.

Quick Cards

Type of Initiative: Problem-Solving

Group Size: You will need at least 12 players for this one.

Playing the Game: (idea source unknown). This one works best when you can have at least two groups of 6-8 players (you can have more than 2 groups playing.) Shuffle the Deck of Cards. After splitting up into small groups, give each player a Card—ask them not to look at the face of the Card just yet. When you say, "GO", each player can look at his or her Card. Then each

group must line up in sequence based on an Ace through King order, as fast as possible. When a team is in the right order they raise their Cards up high together and yell, "DONE!" As the facilitator you can award the metaphorical gold, silver, or bronze medals as they finish (you might have to do spot checks on the order!). After each round, have the groups turn their Cards face down and do a team shuffle—handing the Cards around the group in random order so the values of the Cards are not seen by the players. Then say, "Keep a Card." Each player should have a Card ready for the next round—not looking at it until you say, "GO!" Provide 30 seconds of planning time before each attempt. Play three or four rounds with the smaller teams, then combine two teams together—keeping the same Cards but now shuffling up with both team's Cards—they have the information, how do they share it to make the activity successful. Play a few times for super-speed rating.

NOTE: An interesting shift might occur if players choose to share "verbally" what their Card is as they shuffle—never said they couldn't! This goes along with sharing ideas as well. Will a team share this bright idea with the group (other teams?!).

Debriefing Topics:
• How successful do you think you were at this activity?
• Was there any confusion on where you were supposed to go?
• Did your group share any information with other groups? Why or why not?

~picture smart, logic smart, body smart
Possiblesbag Teambuilding Kit Activity Manual, Chris Cavert

Problem Solving

Facilitator Notes:

 A Little History

At one time, playing cards were taxed, and you can find tax stamps on the packages of some old decks.

Sum of the Group

Type of Initiative: Problem-Solving

Group Size: You will need at least 12 players for this one.

Playing the Game: (idea from Richard McGraw) This one is a bit like **Get 20.**

Remove the face cards from the Deck and spread out the numbered Cards (Aces are the ones) face up on the ground. Divide your group into teams of 3 or 4 and tell them that you will shout out a number, and then say, "Go!" After some possible planning, each group member goes to pick up a number (or 2 if allowed) so that when they either add, subtract, multiply, or divide their numbers they get the number shouted out. Even though you do not mention any competitive aspect of the game, it will most likely show up to talk about. After each team shares their equation with the group, players return their Cards to the circle and another number is called.

NOTE: Spread the Cards out enough so that players have room to move around without stepping on the Cards.

Possibilities: You might limit the equation to only one sign like only adding, subtracting or multiplying. Keep in mind, 2 Cards can be put together to represent one number—the 2 and 4 can be put together to make 24 or 42.

Debriefing Topics:
• How successful do you think you were at this activity?
• How did your group work together to be successful?
• How did your group communicate?

~picture smart, logic smart, body smart
Possiblesbag Teambuilding Kit Activity Manual, Chris Cavert

Facilitator Notes:

♣ A Little History

Margie Golick, a writer on cards, states that Ace means "money", and that the card is traditionally more valuable than the King in card games because the King would be powerless without money. Another account explains that, during the Renaissance, society came to realize that the king exists to serve the people. Therefore, the lowest common man is more powerful than the king, and in cards the ace takes precedence over the King.

Card Punch

Type of Initiative: Problem-Solving

Group Size: Best played with 6 or more players.

Playing the Game: (variation on the activity Key Punch, ideas from Karl Rohnke and Sam Sikes). You can do this one using only the deck of cards and a stopwatch. It is helpful to use some rope or webbing as number barriers.

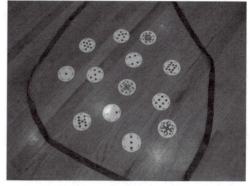

Process: First set up the playing area. If you are using webbing set up two circles on the ground about 25-30 feet away from your starting line. Now set up 2 Card Punch pads. In each webbing circle you are going to set out one suit of Cards—13 cards. For example, the Hearts will go in one circle, each Card facing up spread out equal distance from each other. Then set out the clubs in the other circle—random order spread out within the circle face up. You are ready to play. If you are not using the webbing, simply place each suit grouping about 15 feet away from one another so it is obvious there are two separate card groups.

Have all the players start behind the starting line (this can be an imaginary line or a piece of webbing laid out in a straight line on the floor.) Inform the group that none of the equipment within the activity can be adjusted or moved. Ask the group to divide themselves into 2 equal (or close to it!) teams. One team will be assigned the Hearts and the other the Clubs. On the word "GO!" (the time starts) all the players will go to their respective Card group and as a team they must touch the Playing Cards in order starting with the Ace ending with the King. Only one player can be within the Card group/circle at a time. If there are ever 2 players within the circle the time is void for the entire group. The whole group (2 teams) is going for the lowest possible time. So, when the last player steps across the start/finish line the time stops. Untimed planning can only be done behind the start/finish line—this does not mean that the players cannot take a very long time trial as they plan their strategy near the Card Groups (but we don't tell them this). This activity will work the best when players and teams share ideas for the best possible process for the best time.

Card Punch (*Continued*)

NOTE: Cards do not tend to stay in place during high winds!

Possibilities: For a more challenging run, place 2 suits of Cards into each Card group/circle. If you need to make 3 groups, use another suit to create another Card Punch pad.

Debriefing Topics:

- How successful do you think you were at this activity?
- Was there any confusion on where you were supposed to go?
- How did timing the activity make a difference in your performance?

Facilitator Notes:

~picture smart, logic smart
Possiblesbag Teambuilding Kit Activity Manual, Chris Cavert

Three-Card Line Up

Type of Initiative: Problem Solving

Object of the Game: To line up in the correct order from the lowest number to the highest number.

Group Size: 6-12 Players per deck of cards.

Setting Up the Cards: Remove all of the face cards and tens. Shuffle the deck well.

Playing the Game: Deal each participant three cards. After looking at the cards, participants turn their cards face down and mix them thoroughly so they have no idea of the relative positions of the cards. Then, without looking at the cards, the participants each raise the three cards and hold them to their foreheads, creating a three-digit number, visible to their teammates. Without talking, each participant looks at his teammate's exposed cards. Each participant should place themselves in a line, based on what he believes the position of his own three-digit number. Gesturing is not allowed. After everyone is standing in a line, players may look at their cards. The goal is to get the entire group in the correct order from lowest to highest based on intuition.

Tips for Good Play: The Player, knowing the three digits in his number, but not what place each occupies, may be able to calculate the probabilities of his relative position. If the Player's digits are, for example, 3, 7, and 8, and opponents' numbers are 452 and 921, Player is twice as likely to be in the "middle" (with 7 or 8 in the 100's place) than "low" (with 3 in the 100's place). If Player goes second or third, and other players have already made bets, Player is in an even better position to make a guess that takes the opponents' reasoning into consideration.

Variation: Players do not see their own cards, but they are told the total of their three cards. With only that information and the view of each of the opponents' three-digit number, players each guess whether their number is highest, lowest, or in the middle.

Learning Skills: Practice in reading three-digit numbers, place value, calculating probabilities, deductive reasoning.

Practical Applications: This is a good activity for groups or individuals struggling to find their 'place' in an organization or classroom.

Debriefing Topics:
• What strategies did you use to determine what number you had on your forehead?
• How did it feel to have no help from your teammates?
• What do you want to remember about this activity?
• How can you apply this to what happens everyday in this company/classroom?

Facilitator Notes:

♣ A Little History

You may enjoy collecting cards from other countries and places you or thoughtful friends travel. Souvenir cards often have scenes on the front or back. And some cards have suit markings that reflect local traditions. In Germany, hearts, bells, acorns, and leaves replace the usual hearts, diamonds, clubs and spades. In Spain and Portugal, the suits are swords, batons, coins, and cups. In Switzerland you'll find shields, bells, acorns, and flowers. You may also find letters that abbreviate the names of court cards in the language of the country, like the French R or roi for "king," D or dame for "queen," and V or valet for "jack."

♣

~self smart, logic smart, body smart, picture smart

Blind Line Up

Type of Initiative: Problem Solving

Aim of the Game: To line up in the correct order from the lowest number to the highest number without talking and with their eyes closed.

Group Size: 6-10 Players per suit

Setting Up the Cards: Remove all of the face cards. Aces have a value of 1. Shuffle the deck well.

Playing the Game: Each participant is asked to take a Card, look at the number and put it in their pocket. Ask them not to share their number with anyone else in the group. Distribute blindfolds to those participants who have trouble keeping their eyes closed. The objective is for the participants to line up in order from lowest number to the highest number with their eyes closed, and without talking. They may not strategize before beginning. Inform them that they must be able to prove to themselves and to you the facilitator that they are in the right order before the activity is over. Encourage the participants to put their 'bumpers up' or hands in front of them to avoid any collisions with other participants. Also let them know that you will be watching the group so that no one wanders off from the group and that you will keep them safe. Anytime you ask someone to close their eyes you should do a safety talk about boundaries and safe environments.

Most of the time groups will start out by milling about trying to tap their number out on someone's shoulder. Eventually someone will figure out clapping their number so that they can be communicating with more than one person at a time. If the group gets pretty close but are not quite there it is good to ask for a show of hands if they think they are right before they open their eyes. You can give them feedback such as, "There is one person that does not think the group is in the right order, how can you prove to the group that you are in the correct order?" Usually this will result in one more round of sequential clapping to prove that they are in the right order.

Variation: Remove the Ace card from the cards you hand out. In American society, we are taught to always look for number one. Sometimes this will throw off the group, specifically the number 2 as they will be looking for the Ace card to stand next to.

Debriefing Topics:
- How did you try to communicate your number to the group?
- What was frustrating about this activity?
- How did it feel to have your eyes closed?
- How did other's behaviors in the group affect your performance?

Problem Solving

Trust

Facilitator Notes:

♣ A Little History

Harvard mathematicians say that seven ordinary shuffles are necessary to guarantee that cards are thoroughly mixed.

~body smart, logic smart, music smart

Card Towers

Type of Initiative: Problem-Solving

Props Needed: Deck of Cards and a stopwatch.

Playing the Game: This plays well with 3-24 players. Create groups of 3 or 5 players and give each group 10 Cards (more if you have enough Cards—each group should have the same number of Cards). You will give the groups 5 minutes to plan on how they are going to build the highest free-standing Card Tower with the resources they have—in 30 seconds. Cards may not be creased in any way and no other resources can be used in the tower construction. Score will be determined by multiplying the number of levels by the highest numbered Card at the uppermost level. So, if  there were 3 levels and a 9 was showing at the top level the score would be. . . . . .? After the first round give the groups 3 minutes to plan before the next round. After the second round give them 2 minutes to work out the bugs and go again. The challenge here is how the groups/individuals define the word "tower." Have they even questioned the definition of tower? Could 8 cards lying on top of one another and 2 more set up in a teepee shape on top of the other Cards be considered a tower? Would it be 9 levels times the highest Card in the teepee? Just asking.

Variations: Give some groups more Cards than other groups. What if you only gave them 15 seconds to build? What about 10 or 15 seconds?

Debriefing Topics:
• How successful do you think you were at this activity?
• Did stress play a factor into your success?
• How did timing the activity make a difference in your performance?

~logic smart, body smart
Possiblesbag Teambuilding Kit Activity Manual, by Chris Cavert

Problem Solving

Problem Solving

Facilitator Notes:

♣ A Little History

*Some casinos have been known
to serve refreshments—like
sandwiches, raw veggies, cookies,
or candies—in the shape of clubs,
diamonds, hearts, and spades.*

Insanity Poker

Type of Initiative: Problem-Solving

Group Size: This game plays best with 4 groups—4 to 6 in a group.

Props Needed: Jumbo Deck of Cards and 4 webbing circles. The knowledge of Poker hands is essential, too.

Playing the Game: (Insanity idea from Sam Sikes)

Process: Place the webbing circles in the playing area, each circle will represent the corner of a large square. Webbing circles should be at least 25 feet from each other—so the sides of the square are about 30 feet. In the center of the square area set out the Playing Cards face down and spread out a bit. Divide your group into 4 teams and have each team stand behind a webbing circle, designated as their Home circle—the circle is in between the team and the pile of Cards. At this point you might need to review the types of Poker hands available and which hands are better than others (if you're real nice you might provide a listing of hands for each team). When there is enough understanding of Poker hands you can start.

The objective is, "To win you have to have the best Poker hand in your Webbing circle when the round is over." Say it just like that. Here's how it plays. Only one member from each team can go and obtain one card at a time. Cards can be obtained from the pile of Cards at the center of the square or from any other circle— players may not prevent someone from obtaining a Card from a circle. Once a player has a Card they must bring it to

their Home circle and place it in the circle face up. Then another member of the team can go get another Card—remember only 1 Card per person. When the facilitator yells, "FREEZE" (a good round is about 90 seconds) all players must stop where they are—any movement or placing of a Card after FREEZE will result in elimination for the team in question. Check the poker hands out—you may find that a pair of 2's could win. Play a few rounds before asking them who is winning. Then ask them if there is a way for everyone to win? Why is that important? (The shift happens when all the teams pile their webbing circles on top of one another and place down a Royal Flush in the Center of the Circles.)

Debriefing Topics:
• How successful do you think you were at this activity?
• Did stress play a factor into your success?
• At what point did you start looking at the activity differently?

Facilitator Notes:

~logic smart, picture smart, body smart
Possiblesbag Teambuilding Kit Activity
Manual, by Chris Cavert

♣ A Little History

The number of possible five-card poker hands is 2,598,960.

Multiplication Rummy

Problem Solving

Type of Initiative: Problem Solving

Group Size: 2-4 players

Aim of the Game: The object of Multiplication Rummy is to be the first to lay down all of your cards.

Setting Up the Cards: One deck of cards with face cards removed.

Playing the Game: There are only two traditional 'sit down' card games in this book. This one and Dominoes. I decided to put them in as they are great Logic Smart activities. These work well for the more cerebral learners or for those learning math functions.

Players agree on what multiplication table they will be playing (such as the six-times multiplication table). As a variation they may agree to play for four deals (complete run-throughs of the deck), start with the six times table and increasing it by one each deal. Deal seven cards to each player. Put the remaining deck in the middle and turn up the top card.

Process: The first player may take the exposed card or the top card of the deck. He must discard a card from his hand, placing it on top of the faceup card. Play continues in this fashion.

Players, at their turn, may lay down a card or combinations of two or three cards, using the numbers to form the digits of numbers that are multiples of the agreed-on number. If, for example, the game is built around the eight-times table, a player may lay down a 6 and a 4, as 64, because $8 \times 8 = 64$.

Tens may be used in two ways: a 10 can be laid out with another card placed across it to indicate that the 10 is being multiplied by that number. Thus, if we were playing, "Eights" (which uses the eight-times multiplication table), a 10 could be played with a 4 across it to stand for 40 ($5 \times 8 = 40$).

Tens can also be used to represent the number 10. For example, in playing "nines," a player might lay down a 10 and an 8 as 108, because $12 \times 9 = 108$. Play continues until one player gets rid of all his cards and is the winner of that deal.

Scoring: To calculate their points, players who lost that round count the cards remaining in their hands and multiply the number by the key number for that deal. So, if they are playing "Eights," then the number is 8. The overall winner is the player with the lowest number of points at the end of four deals.

Problem Solving

Suggestion: For very young children who do not know their multiplication tables, have the tables available, or provide the player who needs it with a calculator. The repetition provided by playing will help make these multiplication facts automatic.

Facilitator Notes:

~logic smart, people smart
Source: Card Games for Smart Kids, Margie Golick, Ph.D.

Dominoes

Type of Initiative: Problem Solving

Aim of the Game: Be the first to use up all your cards by playing them onto the layout.

Group Size: 2-6 players

Playing the Game: There are only two traditional 'sit down' card games in this book. This one and Multiplication Rummy. I decided to put them in as they are great Logic Smart activities. These work well for the more cerebral learners or for those learning math functions.

Process: Cut the cards to select a dealer; the player who draws the lowest card gets the job. The entire deck of 52 cards is distributed as evenly as possible between the players. Any inequity will be redressed providing the deal rotates for each hand.

The player to the left of the dealer leads off but must play a seven to start the game. If he or she doesn't have a seven, thy must 'knock' and the turn passes around the table in a clockwise direction.

Once a seven has been played, the next player must try to play onto that card and build up the layout. If the game had commenced with the first player laying a seven of diamonds, the next player has three choices: build in sequence, playing the six of diamonds to the left of the seven or the eight to the right; or they can play another seven of a different suit above the opening card.

If a player is unable to add to the layout in any direction, he or she must 'knock' and the turn passes on.

As the game develops, there will be four rows of cards building to the left and right, and players can build on any of these rows in either ascending or descending sequence.

The first player to get rid of all of his cards is the winner. Play continues until only one player is left holding cards.

⌐logic smart, people smart
Source: Card Games for Kids, Adam Ward.

Problem Solving

Facilitator Notes:

 Suits

The four suits (spades, clubs, diamonds, and hearts) that are commonly found in British cards are said to have their origins in France. There are many theories about what each of the various suits represents. On fairly persuasive theory says that each corresponds to one of the four classes of medieval society. The spades, which represent swords or spearheads (weapons of knights), are the aristocracy; hearts stand for the church; diamonds are a sign of the wealthy (apparently the rich had diamond-shaped paving stones above their graves; and clubs, which are said to signify clover (the food of pigs), represent the peasantry.

Box Cards

Type of Initiative: Problem-Solving

Group Size: Plays best with 5 or more players.

Props Needed: Jumbo Deck of Cards and a stopwatch

Playing the Game: Create groups of 5 to 6 players and set each group in there own little area—at least 12 feet from any other group. Deal 13 Cards to each group. Then toss the Card box out into the center between the groups. You will give the groups 3 minutes to plan, without touching their Cards, and then you will say "GO"—the time starts. At this point the groups can pick up their Cards and implement their plan. What they are required to do is line up the Cards in order by rank and like suit, from Ace to King

off of the box—the Ace must be closest to the box, the 2 must be touching the Ace and so on through to the King. When all the Cards are lined up in order the time stops. Record the time and then pick up all the Cards for a shuffle. Ask the players to return to their starting spots. You will then give all the groups 2 minutes to re-tune their plan as you go around to deal each group 13 new Cards. After the next round you give the groups 1 minute to re-tune. What can be their best possible time? Keep in mind, you never told the groups they couldn't plan with each other, move positions, or that the cards could not be moved.

Possibilities: What if, just what if, as you were shuffling the group's Cards before the 3rd round, you secretly (without anyone seeing you) remove a Card from each pile? I'm sure an interesting discussion about CHANGE would erupt/occur?

Problem Solving

Box Cards (*Continued*)

Debriefing Topics:
- What strategies did you come up with as a group?
- How did time affect your performance?
- How was this activity like everyday life?

Facilitator Notes:

♣ A Little History

Old Card Riddle: Why was the Shah of Persia the best Whist player in England? Because the farmers throw down their spades, the gentlemen give up their clubs, and the ladies lose their hearts when they see the Shah's diamonds.

~body smart, logic smart, picture smart
Possiblesbag Teambuilding Kit Activity
manual, by Chris Cavert

Order Puzzle

Type of Initiative: Problem-Solving

Group Size: 2-18 people, There are enough Cards for 3 puzzles—3 groups.

Playing the Game: (idea from Adventure Woods) This little puzzle is nice for down time or to fill in some activity time space—good for small group interaction. You'll need to separate the Cards into 3 sets.

First set: Aces, Jacks, Queen, Kings.

Second set: Twos, Threes, Fours, Fives.

Third set: Sixes, Sevens, Eights, Nines.

Give each group one of the sets and challenge them to solve the puzzle. They will need to create a 4 by 4 grid of Cards, showing face up, where no row or column of the grid has the same suit in it or the same rank (face value). See the picture for a possible answer.

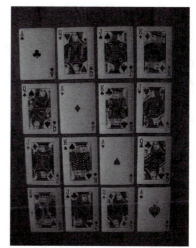

Possibilities: What if the 3 sets of cards were mixed together? How would that change the activity?

Debriefing Topics:
• What was difficult about this activity for you?
• What strategies did you and your team come up with to be successful?
• Were all of the ideas listened to in the group?
• How did you communicate your ideas to others?

~logic smart, picture smart
Possiblesbag Teambuilding Kit Activity manual, by Chris Cavert

Problem Solving

Facilitator Notes:

♣ A Little History

Traditional Fifty-Two Pick Up—Warning to all adults: If a child suggests you play this game, refuse politely. This is not a real game but a time-honored part of the popular culture of childhood. It seems to be passed on by children to children, usually slightly younger—almost as part of an initiation into the world of card playing. One child says to another, "Do you want to play Fifty-Two Card Pick Up?" The unsuspecting victim indicates his willingness. Then the initiator takes a deck of cards, throws them in the air, points to the cards scattered on the floor, and says, "Fifty-Two Card Pick Up!" Having been fooled, the child can hardly wait to find his own victim. I have my older brother Darren to thank for teaching me this game. I apologize to my younger sister Dannon for being my first victim . . .

Number Slide

Type of Initiative: Communication-Cooperation Activity

Group Size: 3-20 people. Three to four groups of 3-5 people works best.

Setting Up the Cards: Separate the cards, (by suit is the easiest way), the Ace-Jack will be used in this activity. Explain that Ace =1 & Jack = 11 in this activity. The cards should be placed on the floor in four rows with three cards each, except for the last row which will only have two cards, (make sure they are NOT in numerical order). If more than one group is doing the activity, I put them all in the same order so all is equal to begin, as most groups become competitive, although that is NOT part of the directions!

Playing the Game:
• The goal of the game is to put the cards in order 1-11 by sliding cards into the empty spot.
• The cards may only slide up/down or left/right, (not diagonally).
• Only one card may be moved at a time.
• Each group member must move at least one card.

Process: Do not answer questions about "which" order. I often put the Ace in the last spot (row 3, spot 3). Most groups spend time moving the Ace to the first row, first spot, (as that is the way we read, so the assumption is that *must* be where to start.)

With three or four groups playing together, at least one group does it a different way, (with the ace in the first row, 4th spot or working vertically, or with an "S" shape). This will lead to great debriefing on the topic of perspective.

Problem Solving

Debriefing Topics:

Communication:

• Why did all groups not come up with the same solution?
• Did the directions say the "order" was 1-11 had to be left to right, top to bottom?

Teamwork:

• Did anyone in the group try to do it a different way? What was the reaction of the group to that person's ideas?

Competition:

• Was it a race?
• In what ways were you competing against other groups?
• How did that add to the pressure?

NOTE: This is like the hand slide typically found as birthday party favors, but using only 12 "slides" versus the 15 slides commonly found.

Facilitator Notes:

~logic smart, people smart, picture smart
Created by Christy Price.

Poker Incentives

Type of Initiative: Associate or Participant Incentive

Group Size: 5 or more

Aim of the Game: To encourage more participation, participants are rewarded with a playing card for their involvement in class or initiative.

Playing the Game: This activity is a good one to use if you are looking for a way to encourage, reward, or motivate your participants. The knowledge of the actual game Poker and what makes a winning Poker hand is essential. The basic fundamentals of the activity are that a participant is rewarded with one card after they have achieved a pre-set goal. After each participant has received 6-10 cards they reveal the best Poker hand they can make with the cards they received. There are many possibilities on how to reward those that participated.

Possibilities:
- Have a prize for the best poker hand at the end of a session.
- Have a prize for the worst poker hand at the end of a session. This illustrates the importance of the reward for participation, not just luck of the draw.
- Before describing the game to participants, do not tell the group there will be a prize for the best poker hand. This is a great way to illustrate intrinsic motivation.
- While describing the game to participants, tell the group there will be a prize for the best poker hand (NOTE: be cautious, as this can encourage too much competition for some groups.)
- Allow 2-5 minutes of negotiation for participants to trade cards with each other to try to get better hands. Works very well with sales associates & competitive managers.

Problem Solving

Examples of On-the-Job Incentives:

- Any staff member receiving a positive customer comment card receives a playing card. At the end of a specified time period, the best poker hand receives a prize.

- Restaurants: for each special or feature meal/promotion sold on a particular evening the server receives a playing card. Best poker hand at the end of the evening receives a prize.

- Hotels: for each "perfectly cleaned" room after inspection, the room attendant, (housekeeper), receives a playing card. Best poker hand receives a prize.

- Sales: for each sale closed over a certain dollar amount, the sales representative receives a playing card. At the end of a specified time period, the best poker hand receives a prize.

Debriefing Topics:

Importance of immediate feedback for staff motivation

- Was it easier to speak up and participate when you were immediately rewarded for the effort?
- Do we acknowledge and praise our staff promptly and publicly?

Value of non-monetary incentives

- Did it matter that the recognition/reward was not monetary?
- Are our staff members motivated by more than money?
- Do we know what our staff values; what motivates them?

Facilitator Notes:

~logic smart, people smart, body smart, self smart
Created by Christy Price.

Team Add vs. Team Subtract

Type of Activity: Problem Solving

Group Size: 4-20 players.

Aim of the Game: The object of the game Team Add vs. Team Subtract is to be the first to reach the desired total (70 for "add" ; 30 for "subtract"). This is a competitive game between two teams. This is a good activity for sales teams.

Value of Cards
All cards have face value.
Jack = 11 points
Queen = 12 points
King = 13 points

Playing the Game: Divide your participants into two teams. Shuffle the deck and give each participant 5 cards. Ask them not to look at their cards. Have each team form a straight line facing the other team. Determine which end of the line is the beginning. Have the first two people from each team face one another. To determine which team is "Add" and which team is "Subtract" have the first person show the card from the top of the deck. The team with the higher card is " Team Add." The team with the low card is "Team Subtract."

Process: Each team begins with a value of 50. Team Add goes first and shows their card. They would add the value of the card played to the number 50. Then Team Subtract would play a card and subtract the value of the card played from the Team Add's new total. Then the second member of Team Add would show their top card and add the value of the card played to Team Subtract's new total. The two teams take turns playing their top cards and adding or subtracting the card's value from the cumulative total. Here is a sample of what might happen in play:

Team	Card Played	Player Says
Add	7	57 (50 + 7)
Subtract	9	48 (57 − 9)
Add	3	51 (48 + 3)
Subtract	King	38 (51 − 13)

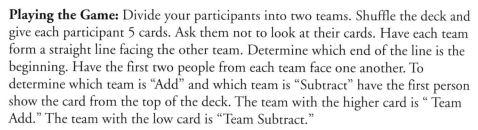

Problem Solving

Scoring: If the total reaches 70, Team Add is the winner. If it falls to 30, Team Subtract is the winner. If the cards run out before there is a winner, reshuffle the cards and give each participant 5 new cards.

Debriefing Topics:
• What was difficult about this activity for you?
• How did competition play a role in the activity?
• How did the winning team treat the team that lost?
• How did the outcomes of this activity relate to similar situations in the office?

Facilitator Notes:

♣ **A Little History**

The number of possible thirteen-card Bridge hands is 635,013,559,600.

~logic smart, people smart, body smart

Partner Find

Type of Initiative: Problem Solving

Aim of the Game: To find your partner without talking and with your eyes closed.

Group Size: 12-40 Players

Setting Up the Cards: Remove all of the face cards. Aces have a value of 1. Shuffle the deck well. This is a Variation of Blind Line Up.

Playing the Game: Each participant is asked to take a Card, look at the number and put it in their pocket. Ask them not to share their number with anyone else in the group. Distribute blindfolds to those participants who have trouble keeping their eyes closed. The objective is for the participants to find 2-3 people with the same number of card they do with their eyes closed, and without talking.

They may not strategize before beginning. Encourage the participants to put their 'bumpers up' to avoid any collisions with other participants. Also let them know that you will be watching the group so that no one wanders off from the group and that you will keep them safe. Anytime you ask someone to close their eyes you should do a safety talk about boundaries and safe environments.

Most of the time groups will start out by milling about trying to tap their number out on someone's shoulder. Eventually someone will figure out clapping their number so that they can be communicating with more than one person at a time.

Debriefing Topics:
- How did you try to communicate your number to the group?
- What was frustrating about this activity?
- How did it feel to have your eyes closed?
- How did other's behaviors in the group affect your performance?

~body smart, logic smart, music smart

Problem Solving

Facilitator Notes:

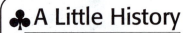

♣ A Little History

The record for the youngest life master in Bridge was set at a tournament in Montreal by Douglas Hsieh, age 11 years, 10 months. Douglas attributed his good intellectual ability to early card playing— particularly games of concentration—when he was just a preschooler.

Team Memory

Type of Initiative: Problem-Solving

Group Size: 5-20 participants

Props Needed: A Deck of Cards (Jumbo cards recommended) and a stopwatch

Setting Up the Cards: Divide your cards into suits. You will need two suits for each group. Shuffle the two suits together and lay them face down on the ground about 15-20 feet away from the group.

Playing the Game: This activity is much like the age-old game of Memory. Divide your groups into small teams of 6-8 people. Establish a starting line and ask groups to stand behind it. Inform the group that they will be timed on their performance. When it is time to begin, participants will go out to the cards one at a time and flip over two cards. If they are a match, they bring the cards back to the group. If they do not match, they turn the cards back over. They are not allowed to move cards around. Establish a base time for the first round. Ask them to set a goal for the second round by how much they would like to reduce their time.

Variations: When the participant is turning the cards over, do not allow them to look at the cards. They can show the cards to their teammates, but they may not look at the cards themselves.

Team Memory (*Continued*)

Debriefing Topics:
- How did your group communicate to one another?
- What was difficult about this activity?
- What did you learn about yourself?
- What strategies did you and your team come up with to be successful?
- Were all of the ideas listened to in the group?
- How did you communicate your ideas to others?
- How did timing this activity affect your performance?

Facilitator Notes:

♣ A Little History

Old, incomplete decks of cards make great invitations to card parties.

~body smart, picture smart, logic smart

Finders Keepers

Type of Initiative: Problem Solving

Group Size: 5 or more

Aim of the Game: The object of the game
Finders Keepers is that players take in cards that
total a predetermined sum.

Point Value of Cards:
Ace = 1 point
Two through ten equal their face value.
Jack = 11 points
Queen = 12 points
King = 13 points

For younger children, all face cards can equal 10 points.

Setting Up the Cards: Lay out all of the cards facedown in 6 rows of 8, with a 7th
row of 4 cards. Establish a starting line about 20 feet away from the cards and ask
the group to stand behind the line.

Playing the Game: Randomly decide who will go first and establish a sequence
order of who will follow that will be maintained throughout the game. The first
player names a number between 2 and 26 and then turns up any two cards. If the
cards total that number, he takes in both cards. If not, he leaves one card faceup and
turns the other over again in its original place.

The next player then turns up two cards and sees if he can make the predetermined
sum with two or more of the faceup cards. If he is successful, he takes in the cards.
If not, he leaves one faceup and turns over the other(s).

When a player succeeds in making the total, he chooses the next number that will be the
sum the players try to make. The activity is finished when all the cards are turned up.

Tips for Good Play: Try to remember the value and location of some of the cards
that have been turned over and replaced. Knowing where a particular number is
located allows a player to go directly to the card needed to complete a total. Before
returning to the group, participants should think carefully about which card they
will leave faceup. They may be able to make it easier for the next player to get the
cards that will equal the total he is after.

Learning Skills: Addition, visual-spatial concepts.

Problem Solving

Finders Keepers (*Continued*)

Debriefing Topics:
- How did your group strategize before sending a member out to the cards?
- What was difficult about this activity for you?
- How did the group communicate?
- Were all of the ideas heard?

Facilitator Notes:

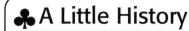

♣ A Little History

There are 15,920,024,220 different hands possible in gin rummy.

~logic smart, picture smart, body smart

King's Corner

Type of Initiative: Problem Solving

Group Size: 6 or more

Props Needed: deck of cards, 15 foot webbing lengths or masking tape.

Setting Up the Game: This activity is much like the traditional adventure activity TP Shuffle with a twist.

Indoors setup: You will need to make a large square with your webbing or masking tape. Each side of the square should be 15 feet long.

Outdoors setup: If you have a low challenge course you can use your TP Shuffle for a group of 13 or less.

Playing the Game: Ask the group to all stand on the webbing. Shuffle your deck and give each participant a card. Participants must not trade cards for the duration of the activity. The group should designate a suit for each side of the square. The King card has to maneuver to the corners. The other cards must line up in order from the King down to the Ace without stepping off of the webbing.

You can create penalties for touches, such as having the entire group start over, or just one person start in their original position. Working together is the key to success.

Debriefing Topics:
• What were some challenges you faced trying to maneuver around each other?
• What were some strategies that you came up with?
• How did you communicate with your teammates?
• What was frustrating for you?

Facilitator Notes:

~body smart, logic smart

Group Gops

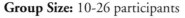

Type of Initiative: Problem Solving, Competition, Consensus

Group Size: 10-26 participants

Competitive Game: How to win: capture the greatest number of cards from the diamond suit.

Setting Up the Cards: Divide your deck as follows: Take out all the hearts—they are not used in this game. Take the diamonds, shuffle them well, and place them in a pile face down between the two groups.

Playing the Game: Divide your group into two teams. Each team is given one suit, either spades or clubs as their hand. It doesn't matter which suit, but they should not be mixed.

Turn the top diamond over and place it face up on the deck of diamonds. Now both teams have a chance to bid for the diamond. Each group comes to consensus on which card they want to bring to the center for bidding. One member of each group brings the chosen card face down to the center.

Simultaneously the players turn over their cards. The higher card (aces are low) wins the diamond. If the spade and club cards bid are of the same value, it is a tie, and neither team gets the diamond in this round. Another diamond is then turned over and the bidding process is repeated. The winner of the second round gets both the diamonds. Once played, the black cards stay in the center; they cannot be reused.

The diamonds are turned over and bid for, until they have all been taken. If there is a tie on the last diamond, when there are no black cards left, roll a dice or toss a coin for heads and tails.

Scoring:

Method 1: The simplest way to score Group Gops is simply to count the number of diamonds gained by each team: the one with the most is the winner.

Method 2: Add the value of each player's diamonds, from 1 (ace) to 11 (jack), 12 (queen) to 13 (king). The first player to reach or pass an agreed total—say, 100—is the winner.

Debriefing Topics:

- How did your individual group come to consensus on which card was going to be taken to the center for bidding?
- Did everyone feel like their ideas were heard in each group?
- How does competition have a place in our workplace/school/group?
- Name some of the feelings you felt while playing this game.

Facilitator Notes:

♣ A Little History

Some of the baffling card tricks done by magicians are done with a "stripper" deck. This is a deck that is very slightly tapered so that one end of the deck is narrower than the other. The difference is hardly visible to the eye, but when a card is reversed in the deck, the magician's fingers can immediately detect it.

~logic smart, body smart, people smart, word smart

Problem Solving

Stop the Clock

Type of Initiative: Problem Solving

Group Size: 12 people

Aim of the Game: To turn over all the cards on the clockface before the fourth King is uncovered. This is a game of fate, so there is a chance the cards will 'win' and not the participants. Frontloading this activity with possible end results is recommended. Plays best with 12 participants as there are 12 numbers on a clockface.

Setting Up the Cards: Shuffle the pack and deal out the cards into 13 piles of four cards each. Twelve of the piles should be set out face down in a circle that approximates a clockface. The remaining set of four cards is then placed in the middle of the layout.

Playing the Game: Invite your group to stand or sit in a circle in positions that would mimic a clockface. Give each participant one pile of cards. Start the game by turning over the top card in the central pile. Suppose the card turned over is a six, you must then place that card face up under the pile of cards at the bottom of the clockface layout (in front of the person in the position that corresponds to six o'clock on a conventional dial).

Having laid down the six, the game is continued by turning over the top card of the six pile. The revealed card is placed under the relevant pile and the top card turned over and relocated to its home.

When the fourth card is revealed in a pile and there is no face-down card left to turn over, you turn over the top card of the next highest pile in the layout.

When have they 'won'? In a traditional card game, they 'win' the game if they manage to get 12 piles of cards on the circular layout faceup. The game is 'lost' if the group turns over the fourth King before they have managed to get the circular layout complete. Simple really—it's the team against the Kings. However, one could argue that if everyone played by the rules, did not sabotage the group, and communicated well, they win every time. These are all good debriefing topics.

Taking Their Time: There's nothing more annoying than getting halfway through a game only to find that you'd earlier put a card in the wrong position. Once the group makes a mistake the game cannot be continued, so encourage them to take their time and do not rush. Younger players may benefit from having a watch or clockface to refer to when playing; alternatively, you might like to draw out the layout on a piece of paper so that they have a model to follow. It is imperative that the cards are spaced evenly, without overlapping, and that the game is played on a flat surface.

Variations: Do the activity silently. Time the activity. Both have very different outcomes.

Debriefing Topics:
- How did the individual roles play a factor in this activity?
- How did you communicate with the group?
- How did the group handle any mistakes that were made?
- How does time affect us every day?
- Did a leader emerge during this activity? If so, who was it and why did you think they were they leader?

Facilitator Notes:

~logic smart, people smart, body smart

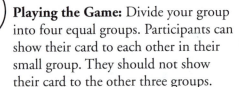

Problem Solving

My Ship Sails

Type of Initiative: Problem Solving

Group Size: 12-28 players

Setting Up the Cards: You will need one card per player. You will need an even number of hearts, diamonds, spades, and clubs. For example, if you have 28 participants, you will need 7 hearts, 7 diamonds, 7 spades, and 7 clubs. Shuffle and deal one card to each player. Put the rest of the deck aside. You will not need it.

Playing the Game: Divide your group into four equal groups. Participants can show their card to each other in their small group. They should not show their card to the other three groups.

The goal of the activity is to have hearts in one group, diamonds in another group, spades in the third group, and clubs in the fourth group. However, the group as a whole may not strategize with one another. Each small group should quietly come to consensus to determine which suit they want to try to be and which participant/card will leave the group each time. When the facilitator says "Go!", all four groups lose a member and gain a member at the same time. Once a member leaves their original group, they are not allowed to speak. This way they do not leak any information or strategies of the other groups.

As soon as one group has all cards of one suit they can say, "My Ship Sails." This lets the other groups know that they have all of the cards they need. This group no longer has to lose or gain a card.

Most groups will think this is a competitive game. They will assume that as soon as their team has all 7 hearts then their team wins. The activity is not over until all participants are in the correct group.

Debriefing Topics:
• How did it feel to leave a group?
• How did your group come to consensus when deciding what card to get rid of?
• Was it difficult not to speak after you left a group?
• How did competition play a role in this activity?

~logic smart, picture smart, body smart, word smart, people smart

Facilitator Notes:

Problem Solving

♣ A Little History

The four Kings have also been said to represent various historical characters. The most popular theory is that the four Kings depicted on the common French-influenced cards are: Charlemagne (hearts), David (spades), Caesar (diamonds), and Alexander (clubs). The Queens are thought to be Judith (hearts), Pallas (spades), Rachel (diamonds) and Argine (clubs). The Knaves (Jacks) are La Hire (hearts), Ogier (spades), Hector (diamonds) and Lancelot (clubs).

♣

Problem Solving

Accountant's Nightmare

Type of Activity: Problem Solving

Group Size: 6 or more

Props Needed: Deck of Cards, possibly some paper, pencils or a calculator.

Playing the Game: Divide your groups into 6-8 people. Shuffle the deck and hand each participant a card. The goal of the activity is to keep your group "out of the red", which means the company is losing money. In an accountant's world, it is always best to be "in the black", which means making a profit. Ask your group to arrange their cards in a numeric equation that will keep them "in the black".

Rules of Play: Red's are negative: Hearts are subtraction, Diamonds are division

Blacks are positive: Clubs are addition, Spades are multiplication

Groups must present their equation to the other groups.

Variation: See how many different equations the group can come up with and still remain "in the black."

Allow the use of a calculator for young players who don't know number facts by heart and who can't make rapid mental calculations.

Debriefing Topics:
• How did your group solve this activity?
• Who seemed to have strong skills in this activity from your group?
• What leadership styles did you see?
• What was difficult about this activity for you?

~logic smart, people smart

Facilitator Notes:

♣ A Little History

The Casino in Caesars Hotel in Atlantic City, New Jersey, reportedly uses 500 decks of cards each day.

Press Ten

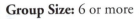

Type of Initiative: Problem-Solving

Group Size: 6 or more

Overview: Press-Ten is a three round game, played in the following way: participants are divided in to 2-4 separate groups. They are placed behind a starting line 15-20 feet from a platform or flat surface. On top of the platform each group has a specific suit of cards, from Ace to Ten, arranged in random order, lying face down. Participants are to send one member across the starting line at a time to flip over the cards in sequence from ace to ten. **Each participant may only flip over one card per trip.** If it is not the next card in sequence they must flip the card back over and return to the group. The first team to flip all ten over in order wins. As soon as the game is over the teams are split up, counting off by four, and the game is immediately started again. On the third round the teams are split up again but allowed to strategize.

Aim of the Game:
> To get people thinking about:
> The roles they play in teams
> The merits and pitfalls of competition
> Why some teams might succeed while others might fail, faced with the same
>   variables—The power of momentum.
> The difference between being able to Brainstorm/Plan versus not.
> The challenges in having to work with many different "teams" throughout a
>   work day.

Setting Up the Cards: Break the deck of cards into suits (diamonds, clubs, spades, hearts) then discard the face cards (jack, queen, king) and set them into four separate piles.

Find an open space with some type of platform in which to spread the cards out FACEDOWN, in four separate rows, in random order. Approximately 15-20 feet from the platform create a "starting line".

Playing the Game:
Explain some variation of the following:

• "In a moment, but not yet, I am going to say: On your mark, Get Set, GO! When you hear "GO!" Your task is as follows: you need to flip your set of cards over, IN ORDER, from ace to ten. Here are the rules."
• Only one person can be across the starting line at any one time.

- If more than one person is over the starting line at anytime, you will have the following consequence . . . (disqualified, they lose a second, etc.)
- Once the person crosses the starting line the team cannot communicate with them in any way.
- That person must proceed to the cards and flip one card, and only one card, over without anyone seeing what card it is. If it is the next card in your sequence, Ace to Ten, you may leave it face up, if it is not, you must return it to the face down position and return to the group.
- You may not rearrange the order of the cards on the platform.
- Every person in the group must flip over a card.
- The first team to get all of their cards flipped over in sequence wins. Ready, Go!
- As soon as the game ends, have your co–facilitators remix the cards and place them face down for another round (turnaround time is critical).
- As soon as they are complete, have the participants count off by fours. Direct that all of the ones are now spades (and direct them to the spade area) all of the twos are hearts, etc. . .
- The moment they reach their new groups call out, "On Your Mark, Get Set, GO!" Do your best not to give them anytime to discuss plans.
- As soon as this round is over, repeat the steps you took to start this round, but this time give them five minutes to come up with a plan amongst themselves.
- After the five minutes of planning, call out, "On Your Mark, Get Set, GO!"
- At the conclusion of this round have everyone circle up for a debrief.

Debriefing Topics:
- Was this challenging, Why?
- Did any of the teams continue to pick up the same card over and over, Why?
- During the second round, How many people deferred to the members of the "winning team" for the second round plan? Why?
- How many people here felt that because they came from a "losing team" they weren't as confident in their input during the second round? Why?

Problem Solving

Press Ten (*Continued*)

- Does winning or losing momentum effect a team's ability to brainstorm or problem solve?
- What was the difference in being able to plan in round three versus no planning in round two?
- Was it difficult to move from team to team, working with your previous competitors?
- Did you feel the same way about your first team as you did you're second or third? Why?
- Was the role that you played in each team the same or different?
- In this context was what was the benefit of competition.
- How much did attitude play in to your success or failure?
- How many people here are members of several different teams just in the context of their work? Are some better than others? Why?

Facilitator Notes:

~body smart, picture smart, logic smart, people smart
Created by Preston Cline, Adventure Incorporated, who wanted an activity named after him, so he created Press-Ten.

Pokerface

Type of Initiative: Problem-Solving, Diversity

Group Size: Plays well with 10 or more.

Playing the Game: There are many playing card activities to deal with inclusion and diversity. Pokerface is one of them. Tell the players you will be handing out a Card to each one of them. Ask them not to look at the face of the Card—at no time during the  game do you want any player looking at the face of her or his own Card. As you explain the directions, ask the participants to hold their Card so the face is down towards the floor. This activity involves the players mingling around the room, holding their Card on their forehead, and treating each other based on the face value of the Cards they are seeing. Kings have the most value in this game and the Ace has the least. The trick here is not to tell anyone what the face value of his/her Card is. Players really want to hang out with the high character Cards—10's and up—and stay away from the low level Cards without actually telling the other players what their Cards are. You can play this game silently or you can allow talking, both ways are powerful.

For example, I'm holding a Card on my forehead (I don't know what my card is but I can see all the Cards of the other players). Now, I want to go hang out with the high Cards—go say "Hello," and , "How's it going? Want to hang out? How about going to the mall later? Have you seen any good movies lately? Did you understand that homework last night?" As I am trying to schmooze with the popular crowd, little to my knowledge, I'm holding a 3 of clubs on my head. Well needless to say, no one is really giving me the time of day. They are all just chatting away with the royalty. Hope you get the idea.

The fun doesn't end there. After some mingling, ask the players to stop talking and stand still—DON'T LOOK AT THE CARDS YET! Tell the group to make a round line—circle (you might want to help them with where "treated well" begins and "treated poorly" ends) in the order of the Card value they think they are. For this game the value is based on how they were treated during the mingling. So, players place themselves within the circle based on how they were treated. When everyone has a place in the circle, ask the participants to look around the room at the order of Cards on each players forehead, then look at their own Card. How did they do? It's amazing to watch the royalty cards get bowed to and the 2 cards get pushed away and treated poorly. Sometimes the 2 cards will form their own 'gang' because they are tired of being treated poorly. Great for discussion on who places value on you. What happens when people feel left out? Isn't the two card sometimes the most valuable card when playing blackjack and you have a 19? The activity is an excellent choice to debrief the concepts of diversity. It is appropriate for people of all abilities.

NOTE: This game can bring up some interesting emotions that you may have to deal with. These are the learning moments! Some learning moments are more powerful than others. Keep a watchful eye over all your players. Make sure they leave the activity with their self-esteem intact.

Debriefing Topics:
• How did it feel to be a Royalty card?
• How did it feel to be a lower numbered card?
• What behaviors did you notice going on in the activity?
• How were you treated?
• Did you notice any secluded groups forming?
• How is this activity like everyday society?

Facilitator Notes:

~logic smart, people smart, picture smart, body smart, self smart
Possiblesbag Teambuilding Kit Activity Manual, by Chris Cavert

Get Into Your Groups

Type of Initiative: Problem Solving and Diversity

Group Size: 12 or more

Playing the Game: Invite your participants to get into a circle. Give each person a card and ask them not to look at it. Inform them that it is a non-talking activity and it should be done in complete silence. Ask each person to put the card to their forehead without looking at their own card. Tell the groups that you are going to be vague with the directions on purpose and then say, "Please get into your groups. Ready, go." There will be some initial confusion as to what 'groups' you are looking for, but people will start milling about and helping each other get into groups based on either number, suit, or color.

It's amazing to watch what groups form and whose idea of a 'group' gets followed. Usually a few people will step forward and start placing people together. Sometimes groups will get started placing people into groups by number, but a larger personality person will jump in with big non-verbal body language and start separating people out with what they think is the 'right answer', by suit or color.

Groups respond very differently to this activity. Some groups are very comfortable with wherever people are 'placed.' Other groups dig deeper into the reality of what is happening. Some individual participants may not 'let' others place them anywhere and choose for themselves what group they want to be in.

This activity should be debriefed well and allow people time to process what happened.

Debriefing Topics:
• How did you get into your groups?
• Who determined what groups you would be in?
• Did the groups change any during the activity?
• Did you agree with the groups that were formed? If so, why? If not, why?
• Were you uncomfortable in the group that you were placed in?
• How is this activity like everyday society? Do we get to choose the groups we are placed in?

~logic smart, people smart, picture smart, body smart, self smart

Facilitator Notes:

♣ A Little History

Cards come in different shapes and sizes. Jumbo cards can be used to demonstrate card games to a group. Tiny cards fit small hands or airplane trays. There are even teeny cards made for doll houses. Round decks can be fun, or they can be used, as a friend once suggested, for coasters. There are decks shaped like fish, Easter eggs, and many other shapes.

Marriage

Type of Initiative: Problem Solving and Diversity

Group Size: 10 or more

Aim of the Game: The object of the game Marriage is find the person who has the same color and number card without saying what card you have.

Setting Up the Cards: This activity works best with an odd number of players. You will need one card for each participant. You will need a pair of cards in the same color and denomination (e.g. three of hearts and the three of diamonds, five of spades and the five of clubs). You will also need one Joker.

Playing the Game: Each participant is given a card and asked not to show it to anyone. The goal of the activity is to find the person in the room who has the same color and number of card as they do. For example, if a participant has the three of hearts, they will be searching for someone in the room that has the three of diamonds. **However, participants are not allowed to say the color or number of their card**. As they mingle from person to person they must describe their card without saying the 'taboo' words of "red" or "three." One might say, "I have an Apple colored card and my car doesn't work well right now as it is missing a tire." When pairs think they have found one another they link arms and wait until the other participants have finished.

There is only one Joker in the room. This person will mingle for the duration of the activity and not be able to find a partner. "Pas de marriage," in French means, "no wedding", hence the title of the activity.

Variation: Do not allow participants to look at their cards. Ask participants to place the card to their forehead and without talking pair each other up according to color and number.

Interesting Story: This activity was played one time using the rules in the Variation. Without talking participants were pairing people up according to color and number. The participant with the Joker was unaware that they had the Joker card or that there was a Joker card being used as there were no other Jokers visible. Other participants were trying to be helpful trying to communicate to this participant what their card was. They were gesturing to this participant by pointing and laughing at them. They were trying to communicate that they had the Joker card, but what came across to the participant was mean and hurtful communication. This participant believed that since she could not find a partner that others were pointing and laughing at her. There was an amazing debriefing session afterwards about nonverbal communication and intention.

Debriefing Topics:
- How did it feel to be the Joker? How did others treat you when they realized you did not have the same card as they did?
- What did it feel like when you found your partner?
- Did you attempt to help others once you found your partner? Why or why not?
- How is this activity like modern society?

Facilitator Notes:

~logic smart, people smart, body smart
Reference: Idea from Margie Golick, Card Games for Smart Kids.

Rejection

Type of Initiative: Diversity, Get to Know You

Group Size: 20 or more

Playing the Game: (idea from Neil Mercer) This activity should be played simultaneously with a variation of **Card Mixers**. Give each participant a card. Ask them to find a partner with a card that has something in common with their card. (this could be the suit, the number, or the color). You could have them discuss several things. Here are a few suggestions:

Get to Know You Topics:
• Find three things you have in common with your partner
• Share a goal you have for the day
• Share why you came to the program/workshop
• Discuss your favorite foods
• Describe the first car you ever owned

What makes the game of Rejection different from the activity Card Mixer is, as you hand out the cards, the participants that receive a red card are given normal instructions for the activity. Participants that are given a black card are given the same instructions and also told they are not allowed to talk to anyone with a red card.

With large groups there are many options for everyone to mill around and find a partner to discuss the chosen topic.
At first those with red cards may be unaware that there are participants in the group that are not allowed to talk to them. After 5 minutes, nonchalantly start exchanging red cards with black cards and give the new instructions to these participants. As the milling about continues there will be visible moments of participants with black cards avoiding the participants with red cards. Stop the activity after this is seen a few times and ask the group to get into a circle to debrief what happened. Always inform the group of the two sets of rules that were being played so the participants with red cards understand that they were avoided on purpose.

Diversity

Getting to Know You

Debriefing Topics:
- How did this activity make you feel?
- How did it feel to have a black card? What were some of your strategies for encounering a participant with a red card?
- If you had a red card, describe an interaction you attempted to have with a black card.
- How is this activity like society?

Facilitator Notes:

♣ A Little History

Playing cards were used for over 300 or 400 years without indices for denominations (A, K, Q, J, or numbers) and without suit symbols in the corners. Cards had to be read full front to figure out their suit and value. Corner indices were introduced in the 19th century for poker players. New decks with these indices were called "squeezer decks" because the indices allowed players to squeeze cards in the hand together and still read the cards.

~logic smart, people smart, picture smart, body smart, self smart

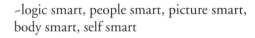

Old Maid or Old Mister

Type of Activity: Problem Solving and Diversity

Group Size: 17-35 players

Aim of the Game: To avoid getting the Old Maid or Old Mister card.

Setting Up the Cards: If you want to play Old Maid, take out all the Queens except the Queen of Spades. If you want to play Old Mister, take out all the Jacks except the Jack of Spades. This is much like the traditional Card game Old Maid.

You will need an odd number of people to play the game. Separate the deck into suits. Set aside the Spades and one other suit. You will need pairs of cards and one card per participant. For example, if you have 17 players you would need the following cards: one Jack of Spades, two 3's, two 4's, two 6's, two 8's, two 9's, two 10's, two Queens, and two Kings.

Playing the Game: Divide the group into four teams. Deal each participant a card. They are allowed to show their card to the members of their small group, but not to the other three groups. Each group looks for pairs in their small group. If a group has any pairs, those two people may sit down. They are still allowed to participate and strategize with their group, but they may not be selected from other groups.

Designate which group will start. The first group chooses one person/card from the group to their left. The person selected leaves their original group and joins the group that chose them. This group looks at the new card that has joined their group. If they can make a pair with the new card, the people with the pair may sit down.

The group who just lost a member is the next group to select a new member from the group to their left. If they can make a pair with the new card, the people with the pair may sit down. If not, the next team chooses their new member.

Now remember, there is one card out there that no one wants, the Old Mister. It may be hard for groups to mask who has this card. Especially if this card gets chosen by another group. Most groups have a hard time disguising their reactions and feelings when the Old Mister joins their group. Likewise, the group that knows the Old Mister has just left their group also has a hard time masking their reaction to this event. One way to spice up the activity so no one knows who has the Old Mister or the Old Maid is to have the participants hold their cards face down and trade cards with three people in their small groups before the next round begins. This way it is a surprise to everyone as to what card is leaving the group.

Problem Solving

Diversity

Another thing to consider is the feelings of the person who has the Old Mister card. There will be many topics that come up in this activity for you to debrief the group with after it is over.

The activity continues until the only person left standing is the Old Maid or the Old Mister.

Debriefing Topics:
- How did it feel to be the Old Maid or the Old Mister?
- How many different people experienced the Old Maid card?
- How did groups treat you when you entered their group as the Old Mister?
- Give examples of how is this like everyday life?
- How often do we exclude people we do not want in our 'group?'
- Have you ever been the only person of your race in a classroom/group?
- How did that make you feel? How can you compare that to this activity?

Facilitator Notes:

♣ A Little History

Japanese cards, called Hanafuda cards, are unusually beautiful. They consist of 48 cards, each depicting a flower. The flowers are grouped in sets of four, each set representing a month. The cards are usually very small, with stenciled or enameled designs and black, glazed cardboard backs.

~logic smart, people smart, body smart, self smart, picture smart

Problem Solving

Diversity

Deck of Card Debrief

Type of Initiative: Processing

Group Size: 4-8 per group

Props needed: A Jumbo deck of playing cards, Playing cards, primarily non-face cards, and those between one (ace) and five, are best.

Aim of the Game: The benefits of this activity are that it is less threatening for participants to speak to just one person at a time rather than the whole group. Sometimes participants are more open if they aren't speaking to their facilitator. Remember good processing can happen even if the facilitator is not present to hear it! This is a useful activity not only to process a specific experience but is great as a closing activity for a session or program day.

Variation #1: Designate a meaning to each suit within the deck of cards. For example hearts could represent feelings, spades could represent situations individuals had a difficult time with, diamonds could represent successes and clubs could represent something they noticed about one of the other group members.

JUMBO PLAYING CARDS

Shuffle the deck and deal each individual a hand (up to 8 cards). For each card, the individual shares with the group an example of what the suit represents. The numbers on the cards and face cards can be involved also. For example, Jacks are wild cards that can be traded for another card in the deck and the numbers on the cards represent how many thoughts that individual may share with the group, etc. You may want to "stack the deck" with specific cards or adapt the rules so that the person who draws a "10" does not have to share 10 items—this could get a bit lengthy!

Variation #2: At the completion of the activity, the facilitator passes out a playing card to each participant. The suit of each card describes the category of your response, and the number shown on the card identifies the number of ideas you need to share on this subject. For example, a four of spades, suggests mentioning four things related to new thoughts that you dug up during the activity.

♥ Hearts: generate conversations about something from the heart.

♣ Clubs: describe things that grow (new ideas, new thoughts, a new point of view)

♠ Spades: are used to dig in the garden, and describe planting some new ideas or things that you dug up during the activity.

◆ Diamonds: are gems that last forever. What are some of the gems of wisdom you gathered during this activity.

Facilitator Notes:

~logic smart, people smart, picture smart, body smart, word smart
A Teachable Moment, Cain, Cummings, Stanchfield, pg 172.
Reflective Learning, Sugerman, Doherty, Garvey, Gass. pg 66.

What You Say 2

Type of Initiative: Processing

Group Size: 2-12 per group

Props Needed: A Jumbo deck of playing cards, primarily non-face cards, and those between one (ace) and five, are best. You also might want to split your group in half if you have more than 12.

(idea shared at the TERA conference)

Playing the Game: You can play What You Say in a number of different ways (another way is listed in the Get To Know You Section). The basic idea is to deal one Card to every player in the group. Then each player will give the number of responses to the question asked that is equal to the number on their Card. You can use the Aces as wild cards—Players can give as many responses (up to the highest card given out) as they want. For example, ask each player to give positive feedback to as many people in the group as the number indicated on their card or, if the number they have is 3, say 3 things you want to remember about the activity.

Possibilities: You could use the face cards for relationship questions.

Kings: talk about some of the leadership qualities you observed.
Queens: talk about some of the helping behaviors you noticed.
Jacks: talk about a set-back you noticed during the activity.

~people smart, picture smart, self smart, word smart
Possiblesbag Teambuilding Kit Activity Manual, Chris Cavert

Processing

Facilitator Notes:

♣ A Little History

Cards were played on the ships sailed by Christopher Columbus and Spanish explorers. They taught card games to the Natives in Central America and North America. Native Americans made cards of animal hides and painted them in the Spanish style.

An Internet Story

This story was forwarded to me through email one day. I thought it might be helpful for anyone working with a Christian group.

It was quiet that day, the guns and the mortars, and land mines for some reason hadn't been heard. The young soldier knew it was Sunday, the holiest day of the week. As he was sitting there, he got out an old deck of cards and laid them out across his bunk.

Just then an army sergeant came in and said, "Why aren't you with the rest of the platoon?" The soldier replied, "I thought I would stay behind and spend some time with the Lord." The sergeant said, "Looks to me like you're going to play cards." The soldier said, "No, sir. You see, since we are not allowed to have Bibles or other spiritual books in this country, I've decided to talk to the Lord by studying this deck of cards." The sergeant asked in disbelief, "How will you do that?"

"You see the Ace, Sergeant? It reminds me that there is only one God. The Two represents the two parts of the Bible, Old and New Testaments. The Three represents the Father, Son, and the Holy Ghost. The Four stands for the Four Gospels: Matthew, Mark, Luke and John. The Five is for the five virgins that were ten but only five of them were glorified. The Six is for the six days it took God to create the Heavens and Earth. The Seven is for the day God rested after making His Creation. The Eight is for the family of Noah and his wife, their three sons and their wives - the eight people God spared from the flood that destroyed the earth. The Nine is for the lepers that Jesus cleansed of leprosy. He cleansed ten, but nine never thanked Him. The Ten represents the Ten Commandments that God handed down to Moses on tablets made of stone. The Jack is a reminder of Satan, one of God's first angels, but he got kicked out of heaven for his sly and wicked ways and is now the joker of eternal hell. The Queen stands for the Virgin Mary. The King stands for Jesus, for he is the King of all kings. When I count the dots on all the cards, I come up with 365 total, one for every day of the year. There are a total of 52 cards in a deck; each is a week - 52 weeks in a year. The four suits represent the four seasons: Spring, Summer, Fall and Winter. Each suit has thirteen cards - there are exactly thirteen weeks in a quarter. So when I want to talk to God and thank Him, I just pull out this old deck of cards and they remind me of all that I have to be thankful for."

The sergeant just stood there. After a minute, with tears in his eyes and pain in his heart, he said, "Soldier, can I borrow that deck of cards?"

~author unknown.
Thanks to my wonderful friend, Larry McPherson for sending me this story.

About Michelle Cummings

Michelle is the owner and creator of her business Training Wheels. She has been in the Experiential Education field since 1993 and has devoted her business to being a creative resource for facilitators and working teams. Training Wheels is a leader in the training and portable equipment industry and prides itself in creating quality, affordable activities, books, and trainings for those seeking experiential resources. Michelle actively seeks and/or creates new activities to enhance her workshops and to provide new resources for facilitators and educators.

Michelle is the co-author of *A Teachable Moment, a Facilitator's Guide to Activities for Processing, Debriefing, Reviewing, and Reflection* along with Dr. Jim Cain and Jennifer Stanchfield. She also authored, *Bouldering Games for Kids, an Educators Guide to Activities for Traverse Walls.* Michelle is working on four other titles as well.

Please sign up for her free e-newsletter at www.training-wheels.com for announcements on when these publications will be available and for other valuable activity ideas.

Michelle received her Bachelors degree in Psychology from Kansas State University, and her Masters degree in Experiential Education from Minnesota State University, Mankato. Michelle grew up on a farm in Norton, Kansas and currently makes her home in Littleton, CO with her husband, Paul, and her two sons, Dawson and Dylan.

Contact Information:

Michelle Cummings
Owner/Trainer/Big Wheel
Training Wheels
7095 South Garrison Street
Littleton, CO 80128
ph. 888.553.0147
ph. 303.979.1708
fax. 888.553.0146
michelle@training-wheels.com

Training Wheels

Workshops and Training Events

Here is a collection of some of my favorite workshops, conference presentations, and training events. You can request any of these prepared programs or a custom designed program.

Processing Workshop: Need more to processing than sitting in a circle, asking questions, and talking about what happened? This workshop is designed to introduce you to a multitude of different processing tools that are simple and easy to use. You will learn how to make/do the activities yourself or find out where to get them. You can increase the quality and value of your programs through powerful reflective learning. One hour to two day workshops available.

Facilitator Training: Join Training Wheels staff and your co-teammates for a facilitator program that will be like none other you have participated in. This experience enhances the foundational skills necessary for facilitators. Most of the training is all hands-on and experiential. Each participant will get the opportunity to facilitate their own activity to receive constructive feedback from the group. 4 day training, 8 person minimum.

Corporate Challenge: We custom design all of our corporate development programs. All programs delivered with an experiential philosophy. Please call with questions and pricing information. One hour to multi-day programs available.

Staff Training and Train the Trainer Programs: Half day to 3 day programs available. We custom design this program to meet your unique needs. We can teach everything from energizers and ice breakers to engaging problem solving initiatives.

Contents Training: If you purchase one of our Teambuilding kits, we offer a Contents Training to teach you how to facilitate the contents of your kit. One to three day programs available.

Bullying and Diversity Workshops: This workshop is designed to teach you some initiatives that will help participants become aware of they way they treat each other. It will encourage educators to facilitate and work for social awareness and change in their programs, schools, and

communities. This workshop will feature experiential practices of multicultural significance with activities that foster the inclusion of traditionally underrepresented groups. From bullying to diversity awareness to inclusion—this workshop enhance your ever-expanding bag of tricks.

Playing with a Full Deck Workshop: Sometimes the simplest prop can be the best item in your bag of tricks. This workshop is based on the activities in this book and will be jam packed the best experiential activities out there using a simple deck of playing cards. All activities will be hands on and active. Using the philosophies of learning styles and multiple intelligences, the workshop will include activities that tap into each learning style of the participants you willl encounter in your practice. Activities will range in style from diversity, icebreakers, problem solving, communication, debriefing, and social norms. Come prepared to play a lot and learn even more. Jokers welcome. One hour to two day workshops available.